Alive Together

Alive Together

NEW
AND
SELECTED
POEMS

LISEL MUELLER

LOUISIANA STATE UNIVERSITY PRESS
BATON ROUGE AND LONDON
1996

05 04 03 02 01 00 99 98 97   5 4 3 2

Designer: Melanie O'Quinn Samaha
Typeface: Granjon
Typesetter: Impressions Book and Journal Services, Inc.
Printer and binder: Thompson-Shore, Inc.

LIBRARY OF CONGRESS CATALOGING-IN-PUBLICATION DATA
Mueller, Lisel.
    Alive together : new and selected poems / Lisel Mueller.
      p.   cm.
    ISBN 0-8071-2127-4 (cl : alk. paper). — ISBN 0-8071-2128-2
    (p : alk paper)
      I. Title.
    PS3563.U35A79   1996
    811'.54—dc20
                                                              96-23399
                                                              CIP

Poems herein have been selected from *Dependencies* (University of North Carolina Press, 1965), copyright © 1957, 1958, 1959, 1960, 1961, 1962, 1963, 1964, 1965 by Lisel Mueller; *The Private Life* (Louisiana State University Press, 1976), copyright © 1967, 1968, 1970, 1971, 1972, 1973, 1974, 1975, 1976 by Lisel Mueller; *The Need to Hold Still* (Louisiana State University Press, 1980), copyright © 1976, 1977, 1978, 1979, 1980 by Lisel Mueller; *Second Language* (Louisiana State University Press, 1986), copyright © 1980, 1981, 1982, 1983, 1984, 1985, 1986 by Lisel Mueller; and *Waving from Shore* (Louisiana State University Press, 1989), copyright © 1986, 1987, 1988, 1989 by Lisel Mueller. "The Possessive Case" originally appeared in *The New Yorker*. Most of the poems in *Dependencies* were reprinted in *Learning to Play by Ear* (Juniper Press, 1990). The author offers grateful acknowledgment to the editors of periodicals in which new poems in this volume first appeared, some in slightly different form: *Alaska Review*, "The Laughter of Women"; *Black Warrior Review*, "In November," "Things"; *Colorado Review*, "Eyes and Ears"; *Georgia Review*, "Midwinter Notes"; *Gettysburg Review*, "An Afterlife," "Pigeons"; *Indiana Review*, "Why I Need the Birds"; *New Virginia Review*, "Pillar of Salt," "Tears"; *Paris Review*, "Imaginary Paintings," "Mirrors"; *Poetry*, "Heartland," "Immortality"; *Poetry East*, "American Literature," "Place and Time"; *Poetry Northwest*, "Happy and Unhappy Families I," "Happy and Unhappy Families II," "Losing My Sight"; *Quarterly West*, "Paper-White Narcissus"; *Seneca Review*, "Curriculum Vitae," "Night Voyage: A Dream"; *Triquarterly*, "Silence and Dancing"; *Willow Review*, "The Late-Born Daughters"; *Willow Spring*, "Statues." "A Short History of the Rose" was first published in the chapbook *Voices from the Forest* (Juniper Press, 1977). "An Unanswered Question" first appeared in *The Poet's Notebook*, edited by Stephen Kuusisto, Deborah Tall, and David Weiss (W. W. Norton, 1995).

The author wishes to thank the National Endowment for the Arts for a fellowship in 1990 that allowed her to write many of the new poems in the volume, and John Judson, the publisher and editor of Juniper Press, for his support and friendship over many years.

The paper in this book meets the guidelines for permanence and durability of the Committee on Production Guidelines for Book Longevity of the Council on Library Resources. ∞

FOR MY FAMILY; AND FOR MY FORMER STUDENTS,
WITH GRATITUDE FOR THEIR FRIENDSHIP

In Passing

How swiftly the strained honey
of afternoon light
flows into darkness

and the closed bud shrugs off
its special mystery
in order to break into blossom:

as if what exists, exists
so that it can be lost
and become precious

CONTENTS

New Poems

From *Second Language* (1986)

xi

NEW POEMS

I

Curriculum Vitae

1992

1) I was born in a Free City, near the North Sea.

2) In the year of my birth, money was shredded into confetti. A loaf of bread cost a million marks. Of course I do not remember this.

3) Parents and grandparents hovered around me. The world I lived in had a soft voice and no claws.

4) A cornucopia filled with treats took me into a building with bells. A wide-bosomed teacher took me in.

5) At home the bookshelves connected heaven and earth.

6) On Sundays the city child waded through pinecones and primrose marshes, a short train ride away.

7) My country was struck by history more deadly than earthquakes or hurricanes.

8) My father was busy eluding the monsters. My mother told me the walls had ears. I learned the burden of secrets.

9) I moved into the too bright days, the too dark nights of adolescence.

10) Two parents, two daughters, we followed the sun and the moon across the ocean. My grandparents stayed behind in darkness.

11) In the new language everyone spoke too fast. Eventually I caught up with them.

12) When I met you, the new language became the language of love.

13) The death of the mother hurt the daughter into poetry. The daughter became a mother of daughters.

14) Ordinary life: the plenty and thick of it. Knots tying threads to everywhere. The past pushed away, the future left unimagined for the sake of the glorious, difficult, passionate present.

15) Years and years of this.

16) The children no longer children. An old man's pain, an old man's loneliness.

17) And then my father too disappeared.

18) I tried to go home again. I stood at the door to my childhood, but it was closed to the public.

19) One day, on a crowded elevator, everyone's face was younger than mine.

20) So far, so good. The brilliant days and nights are breathless in their hurry. We follow, you and I.

PLACE AND TIME

History is your own heartbeat.
    —Michael Harper

Last night a man on the radio,
a still young man, said the business district
of his hometown had been plowed under.
The town was in North Dakota.
Grass, where the red-and-gold
Woolworth sign used to be,
where the revolving doors
took him inside Sears;
gone the sweaty seats
of the Roxy—or was it the Princess—
of countless Friday nights
that whipped his heart to a gallop
when a girl touched him, as the gun
on the screen flashed in the moonlight.
Grass, that egalitarian green,
pulling its sheet over rubble,
over his barely cold childhood,
on which he walks as others walk
over a buried Mayan temple
or a Roman aqueduct beneath
a remote sheep pasture
in the British Isles. Yet his voice,
the modest voice on the radio,
was almost apologetic,
as if to say, what's one small town,
even if it is one's own,
in an age of mass destruction,
and never mind the streets and stones
of a grown man's childhood—
as if to say, the lives we live
before the present moment
are graves we walk away from.

Except we don't. We're all
pillars of salt. My life began
with Beethoven and Schubert
on my mother's grand piano,

the shiny Bechstein on which she played
the famous symphonies
in piano reductions. But they were no
reductions for me, the child
who now remembers nothing
earlier than that music,
a weather I was born into,
a jubilant light or dusky sadness
struck up by my mother's hands.
Where does music come from
and where does it go when it's over—
the child's unanswered question
about more than music.

My mother is dead, and the piano
she could not take with her into exile
burned with our city in World War II.
That is the half-truth. The other half
is that it's still her black Bechstein
each concert pianist plays for me
and that her self-taught fingers
are behind each virtuoso performance
on the stereo, giving me back
my prewar childhood city
intact and real. I don't know
if the man from North Dakota has
some music that brings back
his town to him, but something does,
and whatever he remembers
is durable and instantly
retrievable and lit
by a sky or streetlight
which does not change. That must be why
he sounded casual about
the mindless wreckage, clumsy
as an empty threat.

IMMORTALITY

In Sleeping Beauty's castle
the clock strikes one hundred years
and the girl in the tower returns to the world.
So do the servants in the kitchen,
who don't even rub their eyes.
The cook's right hand, lifted
an exact century ago,
completes its downward arc
to the kitchen boy's left ear;
the boy's tensed vocal cords
finally let go
the trapped, enduring whimper,
and the fly, arrested mid-plunge
above the strawberry pie
fulfills its abiding mission
and dives into the sweet, red glaze.

As a child I had a book
with a picture of that scene.
I was too young to notice
how fear persists, and how
the anger that causes fear persists,
that its trajectory can't be changed
or broken, only interrupted.
My attention was on the fly:
that this slight body
with its transparent wings
and life-span of one human day
still craved its particular share
of sweetness, a century later.

LOSING MY SIGHT

I never knew that by August
the birds are practically silent,
only a twitter here and there.
Now I notice. Last spring
their noisiness taught me the difference
between screamers and whistlers and cooers
and O, the coloraturas.
I have already mastered
the subtlest pitches in our cat's
elegant Chinese. As the river
turns muddier before my eyes,
its sighs and little smacks
grow louder. Like a spy,
I pick up things indiscriminately:
the long approach of a truck,
car doors slammed in the dark,
the night life of animals—shrieks and hisses,
sex and plunder in the garage.
Tonight the crickets spread static
across the air, a continuous rope
of sound extended to me,
the perfect listener.

An Unanswered Question

If I had been the lone survivor
of my Tasmanian tribe,
the only person in the world
to speak my language
(as she was),

if I had known and believed that
(for who can believe
in an exhaustible language),
and if I had been shipped
to London, to be exhibited
in a cage (as she was)
to entertain the curious
who go to museums and zoos,

and if among all those people
staring and pointing and laughing
and making their meaningless sounds
there had been one thoughtful face,
a woman's, say, sympathetic,

who might have instinctively understood
the one word I could not let die,
the indispensable word
I must pass through the bars
of mutual incomprehension,

what word would it have been?

EYES AND EARS

Perhaps it's my friendship with Dick,
who watches and listens from his wheelchair
but cannot speak, has never spoken,
that makes me aware of the daily
unintrusive presences
of other mute watchers and listeners.
Not the household animals
with their quick bodies—they have cry
and gesture as a kind of language—
but rooted lives, like trees,
our speechless ancestors,
which line the streets and see me,
see all of us. By August
they're dark with memories of us.
And the flowers in the garden—
aren't they like our children were:
tulips and roses all ears,
asters wide-open eyes?
I don't think the sun bothers
with us; it is too full
of its own radiance. But the moon,
that silent all-night cruiser,
wants to connect with us noisy breathers
and lets itself into the house
to keep us awake. The other day,
talking to someone else
and forgetting Dick was in the room,
I suddenly heard him laugh.
What did I say, Dick? You're like the moon,
an archive of utterance not your own.
But when I walk over to you,
you turn into the sun,
on fire with some news
of your own life. Your fingers search
among the words inked on your board,
the few, poor, catchall words
you have, to let me glimpse
the white heat trapped inside you.

PAPER-WHITE NARCISSUS

Strange, how they got their name—
a boy, barely a man,
looked into sunlit water
and saw himself so beautiful
he spent his life pursuing
that treacherous reflection.
There is no greater loneliness.

Here they are, risen
from the darkness of the pebbled pool
we have made for them in a dish—
risen and broken through
the long, green capsules
to show us their faces:

they are so delicate they invite
protection or violation,
and they are blind.

Midwinter Notes

On my shelf of photographs
the dead have come to outnumber the living.
They stand like artificial flowers
among the real ones, so lifelike
even God might be fooled.

*

My husband says spring will be early.
He says this every year,
and every year I disagree.
He needs me, the dark side
of the planetary equation.
Together we make the equinox.

*

As the world grows darker
before my eyes, the sun
sends me sharper, harder
glances off glass, off ice—
like the white light reported
by the temporarily dead,
the brightness they are teased with
and turned away from.

*

Another chance to wake up together,
accepting the invitation
of one more morning. Another chance
to push the black dream of waking alone
over the edge of the world,
where there is no life to sustain me.

*

Only after
our garden became a graveyard
strewn with shriveled leaves
did the white stem rise

from the hermetic bulb,
displaying five lavender petals:
Colchicum autumnale—
a brilliant contradiction,
out of phase, like an angel
strayed into Time, our world.

*

Though I fly, like the crow,
the shortest distance to death,
some knowledge will always remain foreclosed.

*

At twilight, water in roadside ditches
pulls down the last light
to be transformed from lead
into softly gleaming silver.
It has taken me years to discover
this slant conjunction of sky and water
late in the day, when the dead
are allowed their brief shining.

PILLAR OF SALT

More and more I resemble
the woman turned stela,
whom I imagine standing
like a solitary cactus
at the edge of the desert.

By now I too have become
a storage tower of memory,
that salty substance not absorbed
or sloughed off by the body.

Like her, I was rescued
(who knows why) for survival
and looked back at the destruction
of the place I had come from,
stunned by history's genius
for punishing the guiltless.

Surely not all of her people were wicked.
Perhaps the ones who loved her
and whom she loved
were gentle, like my people,
whom I reprieve from their deaths
each time I remember my life
among them, my grandparents,
three guardian angels.

*

As a child I played
with Japanese paper flowers.
In the package they were
tiny, shriveled bits of confetti,
nearly weightless,
but when they were put in a bowl of water
they sprang open, transformed
into a splurge of lotus flowers,
amazing yellow, orchid, rose.

It's like that when I think of them,
when I give them back brilliant moments
of family happiness
in random sunlit spaces.
The show is not for them.
It is for me: I set it up
so I can change the ending,
stop it short of hell,
give them a bearable old age,
a decent death. It doesn't work;
it hasn't worked all these years;
history has taken nothing back.

*

Memory is the only
afterlife I can understand,
and when it's gone, they're gone.
Soon I will betray them.
Think of it as the solid pillar
dissolving, all that salt
seeping back into the sea.

2

STATUES

In Prague, or perhaps Budapest,
the heroes have fallen off their horses.
Here lies a general's profile
and here a helmet, there
a ferrous glove still holding the reins.
The horses, so long inert
under the heavy bodies,
are not used to wind and sun,
nor to the tenderness of their flanks
now that the boots are gone,
and their eyes, so long overcast
by bronze or stone, are slow
to take in the gray city,
the heavyset houses. Gradually
they start to move, surprised
by their new lightness. There's a scent
of rain in the air, and something clicks
inside their heads; it has to do
with green, with pasture. They step down
from their pedestals, unsteady as foals
beginning to walk. No one pays attention
to riderless horses walking
through city streets; these are
supernatural times. Near the edge of town,
where the sky expands, they trust themselves
to break into a run
and then drop out of sight
behind a bank of willows
whose streamers promise water.

The Laughter of Women

The laughter of women sets fire
to the Halls of Injustice
and the false evidence burns
to a beautiful white lightness

It rattles the Chambers of Congress
and forces the windows wide open
so the fatuous speeches can fly out

The laughter of women wipes the mist
from the spectacles of the old;
it infects them with a happy flu
and they laugh as if they were young again

Prisoners held in underground cells
imagine that they see daylight
when they remember the laughter of women

It runs across water that divides,
and reconciles two unfriendly shores
like flares that signal the news to each other

What a language it is, the laughter of women,
high-flying and subversive.
Long before law and scripture
we heard the laughter, we understood freedom.

Pigeons

Like every kingdom,
the kingdom of birds
has its multitude of the poor,
the urban, public poor
whose droppings whiten
shingles and sidewalks,

who pick and pick
(but rarely choose)
whatever meets their beaks:
the daily litter
in priceless Italian cities,
and here, around City Hall—
always underfoot,
offending fastidious people
with places to go.

No one remembers how it happened,
their decline, the near-
abandonment of flight,
the querulous murmurs,
the garbage-filled crops.
Once they were elegant, carefree;
they called to each other in rich, deep voices,
and we called them doves
and welcomed them to our gardens.

Imaginary Paintings

1 HOW I WOULD PAINT THE FUTURE

A strip of horizon and a figure,
seen from the back, forever approaching.

2 HOW I WOULD PAINT HAPPINESS

Something sudden, a windfall,
a meteor shower. No—
a flowering tree releasing
all its blossoms at once,
and the one standing beneath it
unexpectedly robed in bloom,
transformed into a stranger
too beautiful to touch.

3 HOW I WOULD PAINT DEATH

White on white or black on black.
No ground, no figure. An immense canvas,
which I will never finish.

4 HOW I WOULD PAINT LOVE

I would not paint love.

5 HOW I WOULD PAINT THE LEAP OF FAITH

A black cat jumping up three feet
to reach a three-inch shelf.

6 HOW I WOULD PAINT THE BIG LIE

Smooth, and deceptively small
so that it can be swallowed
like something we take for a cold.

An elongated capsule,
an elegant cylinder,
sweet and glossy,
that pleases the tongue
and goes down easy,
never mind
the poison inside.

7 HOW I WOULD PAINT NOSTALGIA

An old-fashioned painting, a genre piece.
People in bright and dark clothing.
A radiant bride in white
standing above a waterfall,
watching the water rush
away, away, away.

Things

What happened is, we grew lonely
living among the things,
so we gave the clock a face,
the chair a back,
the table four stout legs
which will never suffer fatigue.

We fitted our shoes with tongues
as smooth as our own
and hung tongues inside bells
so we could listen
to their emotional language,

and because we loved graceful profiles
the pitcher received a lip,
the bottle a long, slender neck.

Even what was beyond us
was recast in our image;
we gave the country a heart,
the storm an eye,
the cave a mouth
so we could pass into safety.

TEARS

The first woman who ever wept
was appalled at what stung
her eyes and ran down her cheeks.
Saltwater. Seawater.
How was it possible?
Hadn't she and the man
spent many days moving
upland to where the grass
flourished, where the stream
quenched their thirst with sweet water?
How could she have carried these sea drops
as if they were precious seeds;
where could she have stowed them?
She looked at the watchful gazelles
and the heavy-lidded frogs;
she looked at glass-eyed birds
and nervous, black-eyed mice.
None of them wept, not even the fish
that dripped in her hands when she caught them.
Not even the man. Only she
carried the sea inside her body.

Mirrors

After I put on lipstick
I turn my hand mirror upside down.
I know that mirrors can start fires—
and why shouldn't they,
they see too much of us.
Imagine absorbing so much beauty
and so much pain in silence,
involuntary confidantes
like chambermaids with their tongues cut out.
Not a hint of bloodshot eyes
or brilliant acts of cover-up
to anyone. But with us
they're utterly relentless,
since truth is what we ask for—
and how can we expect them
to blur and show us mercy
when the face, that peach or apple,
puckers and blotches, when red and pink
fade like the gorgeous ephemera
of summer? Of course they see
that we grow to hate them;
that's the thanks they get.
No wonder there are times
when it takes only the sun's
intrusive glare to make them explode.

An Afterlife

Now that the king of crime is dead
and the funeral procession of thousands
carrying lilies and carnations
is over, the spinners of legends
are busy, as busy as the three fates
at the threadbare heart of the world.
Already the children in the slums
are clapping their hands to a new chant
about the doves that flew from his mouth
each time he called to them, and their mothers
tell about baskets of food
left on the doorstep. No one remembers
an armored luxury limousine,
but everyone knows that he spoke at his birth,
his own name, clear and strong.
His mother died from the shock
of the miracle, but she died happy.
The people he murdered? Well, they deserved it;
they were his enemies, they were the law,
and not a single, stiff, cold hand
has broken through any grave
and pointed straight up to heaven.
Numerous sightings of him,
larger than life, are being reported
by people out after midnight.
Girls who put roses on his grave
come home with feverish faces
and stories of freshly disturbed ground.
"It's true," they whisper, "see for yourself."

HEARTLAND

Now that we've given our hearts away
with the bric-a-brac, we want them back.
Now we look for them secondhand,
someone else's, in the old songs,
the slowly unfolding novels
we never had time for. Hearts
that taught themselves to fly;
riddled hearts, neatly punctured
by their owners' accurate pistols;
overstuffed hearts, still leaking
downy secrets like feathers.

We want to hear someone say,
"I give you my heart," meaning,
"summer and winter," meaning,
"all my time in this world,"
and to imagine what it is like,
dying of heartbreak,
a subtle, yet extravagant death,
nothing to do with the blood supply,
or lack of it, that kills us.

How lucky they were, with a safe place
for their volatile passions!
When did we enter the heartless age?
From some anonymous ceiling
a speaker blares, "Mon coeur, corazón,
Dein ist mein ganzes Herz."

Poets and storytellers
move into the vacancies
Edward Hopper left them.
They settle down in blank spaces,
where the light has been scoured and bleached
skull-white, and nothing grows
except absence. Where something is missing,
the man a woman waits for,
or furniture in a room
stripped like a hospital bed
after the patient has died.
Such bereft interiors
are just what they've been looking for,
the writers, who come with their baggage
of dowsing rods and dog-eared books,
their uneasy family photographs,
their lumpy beds, their predilection
for starting fires in empty rooms.

Silence and Dancing

"Schweigen und tanzen" are words spoken by Elektra
near the end of the opera by Richard Strauss and Hugo
von Hofmannsthal.

Silence and dancing
is what it comes down to
in the end for them,
as they struggle from wheelchair to bed,
knowing nothing changes,
that the poor, who are themselves,
will become even poorer
and the fatuous voices on the screen
will go on gabbling about another
war they cannot do without.

What defense against this
except silence and dancing,
the memory of dancing—

O, but they danced, did they ever;
she danced like a devil, she'll tell you,
recalling a dress the color of sunrise,
hair fluffed to sea-foam,
some man's, some boy's
damp hand on her back
under the music's sweet, hot assault

and wildness erupting inside her
like a suppressed language,
insisting on speaking itself
through her eloquent body,

a far cry
from the well-groomed words on her lips.

THE LATE-BORN DAUGHTERS

The late-born daughters of famous fathers,
who never knew their fathers
except to sit on their laps
when they visited once or twice,
go up to the attic to read
the brilliant and cruel letters
their mothers kept until they died.

The younger daughters of famous fathers,
born of the late, last marriages,
who watched their mothers grow tongue-tied
when they spoke about their fathers,
go to the library archives,
sign in, sign out, for permission
to search for their missing fathers.

The soft-spoken daughters of famous fathers,
who long since changed their names
and do not answer their phones,
collect the lives of their fathers,
their dead, difficult fathers,
in stories told by neighbors and lovers
and servants and hangers-on.

The aging, late-born, younger daughters
spend the best years of their lives
with their haunted, shipwrecked fathers.
They iron their fathers' shirts,
they cradle their heads in their laps,
they keep their desperate secrets,
they sit up all night with their fathers.

Happy and Unhappy Families I

If all happy families are alike,
then so are the unhappy families,
whose lives we celebrate
because they are motion and heat,
because they are what we think of as *life*.
Someone is lying and someone else
is being lied to. Someone is beaten
and someone else is doing the beating.
Someone is praying, or weeps
because she does not know how to pray.
Someone drinks all night;
someone cowers in corners;
someone threatens and someone pleads.
Bitter words at the table,
bitter sobs in the bedroom;
reprisal breathed on the bathroom mirror.
The house crackles with secrets;
everyone draws up a plan of escape.
Somebody shatters without a sound.
Sometimes one of them leaves the house
on a stretcher, in terrible silence.
How much energy suffering takes!
It is like a fire that burns and burns
but cannot burn down to extinction.
Unhappy families are never idle;
they are where the action is,
unlike the others, the happy ones,
who never raise their voices
and spit no blood, who do nothing
to deserve their happiness.

Happy and Unhappy Families II

According to the director
even Electra was once a child
in a happy family. Hard to imagine
Agamemnon's daughters
batting balloons across the lawn,
while Orestes shouts
joyfully from his rocking horse
and the soon-to-be-murdered parents
smile fondly over their summer drinks.

Only in the catastrophe,
the inescapable horror show,
do they exist for us,
while close to home, in the latest
double murder and suicide,
horror fails the imagination.
Nothing, a blank. We remember
the good times, study the family pictures.
The little girl had a birthday
last week. They had balloons.
They played jump rope in the yard.
The mother always looked pretty.
He was always polite.

In the play, we know what must happen
long before it happens,
and we call it tragedy.
Here at home, this winter,
we have no name for it.

READER

For Mary Elsie Robertson, author of Family Life

A husband. A wife. Three children. Last year they did not exist; today the parents are middle-aged, one of the daughters grown. I live with them in their summer house by the sea. I live with them, but they can't see me sharing their walks on the beach, their dinner preparations in the kitchen. I am in pain because I know what they don't, that one of them has snipped the interlocking threads of their lives and now there is no end to the slow unraveling. If I am a ghost they look through, I am also a Greek chorus, hand clapped to mouth in fear, knowing their best intentions will go wrong. "Don't," I want to shout, but I am inaudible to them; beach towels over their shoulders, wooden spoon in hand, they keep pulling at the threads. When nothing is left they disappear. Closing the book I feel abandoned. I have lost them, my dear friends. I want to write them, wish them well, assure each one of my affection. If only they would have let me say good-bye.

ANIMALS ARE ENTERING OUR LIVES

"I will take care of you," the girl said to her brother, who had
been turned into a deer. She put her golden garter around his
neck and made him a bed of leaves and moss.
                                                    —from an old tale

Enchanted is what they were
in the old stories, or if not that,
they were guides and rescuers of the lost,
the lonely, needy young men and women
in the forest we call the world.
That was back in a time
when we all had a common language.

Then something happened. Then the earth
became a place to trample and plunder.
Betrayed, they fled to the tallest trees,
the deepest burrows. The common language
became extinct. All we heard from them
were shrieks and growls and wails and whistles,
nothing we could understand.

Now they are coming back to us,
the latest homeless, driven by hunger.
I read that in the parks of Hong Kong
the squatter monkeys have learned to open
soft drink bottles and pop-top cans.
One monkey climbed an apartment building
and entered a third-floor bedroom.
He hovered over the baby's crib
like a curious older brother.
Here in Illinois
the gulls swarm over the parking lots
miles from the inland sea,
and the Canada geese grow fat
on greasy leftover lunches
in the fastidious, landscaped ponds
of suburban corporations.
Their seasonal clocks have stopped.
They summer, they winter. Rarer now
is the long, black elegant V
in the emptying sky. It still touches us,
though we do not remember why.

But it's the silent deer who come
and eat each night from our garden,
as if they had been invited.
They pick the tomatoes and tender beans,
the succulent day-lily blossoms
and dewy geranium heads.
When you labored all spring,
planting our food and flowers,
you did not expect to feed
an advancing population
of the displaced. They come,
like refugees everywhere,
defying guns and fences
and risking death on the road
to reach us, their dispossessors,
who have become their last chance.
Shall we accept them again?
Shall we fit them with precious collars?
They scatter their tracks around the house,
closer and closer to the door,
like stray dogs circling their chosen home.

Why I Need the Birds

When I hear them call
in the morning, before
I am quite awake,
my bed is already traveling
the daily rainbow,
the arc toward evening;
and the birds, leading
their own discreet lives
of hunger and watchfulness,
are with me all the way,
always a little ahead of me
in the long-practiced manner
of unobtrusive guides.

By the time I arrive at evening,
they have just settled down to rest;
already invisible, they are turning
into the dreamwork of trees;
and all of us together—
myself and the purple finches,
the rusty blackbirds,
the ruby cardinals,
and the white-throated sparrows
with their liquid voices—
ride the dark curve of the earth
toward daylight, which they announce
from their high lookouts
before dawn has quite broken for me.

A Short History of the Rose

"You will know me
by the rose
in my left hand,"
a woman writes
in a secret letter.
"The others
will carry daisies.
Everything
is arranged for us."

*

A red bullet
shot from a cannon,
not to hurt,
but to celebrate,

a vowel from
the language of happiness,
a salute.

*

Read the history
of the mouth,
of the womb,

of places
infinitely desired
and female,

if you want to know
the history
of the rose.

*

Thorns were added,
a later invention.
It is not certain by whom:

a bitter lover, or
a poet trying to crash
the party in heaven.

*

It is dusk.
In the garden
the single flower
glows like a woman
awaiting
a special evening.

In November

Outside the house the wind is howling
and the trees are creaking horribly.
This is an old story
with its old beginning,
as I lay me down to sleep.
But when I wake up, sunlight
has taken over the room.
You have already made the coffee
and the radio brings us music
from a confident age. In the paper
bad news is set in distant places.
Whatever was bound to happen
in my story did not happen.
But I know there are rules that cannot be broken.
Perhaps a name was changed.
A small mistake. Perhaps
a woman I do not know
is facing the day with the heavy heart
that, by all rights, should have been mine.

Night Voyage: A Dream

The boatman, a silhouette,
kept his back toward us.

It was night, but the summer sky
held on to its subtle light.
We could see a faint glow
on the water and distinguish
the dark green banks we could almost touch.

We stood in the boat and watched
as it glided past the banks
endlessly, like a phrase
repeated over and over,
though there was no sound,
only the rhythm of absolute silence.

We sat down and held each other,
touched each other once more
in the places of pleasure.
We knew it was for the last time,
and though we understood nothing,
we were not frightened, only entranced.

CAPTIVITY

On February 4, 1974, Patricia Campbell Hearst was ab-
ducted from her apartment in Berkeley, California, by
members of the Symbionese Liberation Army, a group
whose total membership consisted of three men and five
women. She was kept, blindfolded, in a dark, five-foot
closet for fifty-seven days and forced to make several au-
diotapes, which the SLA released in order to extort money
from her parents, purportedly to feed the hungry. She was
given the name Tania.

From the fifty-eighth day on she was allowed to share
the life of the others in their sparse, secret apartment and
subjected to intensive indoctrination. She remained with
the SLA until her arrest on September 18, 1975, and par-
ticipated in at least two bank robberies. On another occa-
sion she sprayed Cranshaw Boulevard in Los Angeles
with bullets from a submachine gun to cover a comrade
apprehended for shoplifting. She did not attempt to es-
cape, even when opportunities presented themselves. In
her book, *Every Secret Thing* (1982), she wrote about this
period, "I had crossed over, and I would have to make the
best of it. To live from day to day, to do whatever they
said, to play my part, and to pray that I would survive."

When Patricia Hearst was arrested, she gave her
occupation as urban guerrilla. She was convicted of
bank robbery and received a prison sentence, which was
commuted by President Jimmy Carter on February 1,
1979.

I

Eight weeks in that closet:
a child's worst nightmare,
being locked up in the dark.
Two nightmares really, the blindfold
making another closet,
and the radio always on,
blaring just out of reach
of her useless hands. So she became
a child again, curled up
or hunched against the dirty wall,
the blindfold always wet
from her compulsive weeping,
her only relief the stumbling
to the bathroom, like a toddler
who is led by a punitive nursemaid.
Once when she tottered out,
she heard birdsong outside the window

47

and knew a season had passed.
Winter was over. The notion of spring
struck her imagination
as something foreign, a fiction.
Green, she said to herself,
a beautiful word in another language,
devoid of meaning.

2

Better to pretend the man
who came to her in the closet
was her lover, instead of remembering
what he was: her captor, jailer;
better not to think of herself
as hostage, booty, prey.
And when they offered her food and water,
she held out as long as she could,
but she wanted to live, as fiercely
as a skinny, abandoned cat
that circles an unknown house
more narrowly each day
until it finally laps up the milk
that gleams in the bowl by the kitchen door,
                                              beckoning.

3   THE TAPES

In the beginning we followed her story
as we used to follow
the girl in the fairy tale.
Pity and fear. The decent girl
cast out to be cruelly tested
in the dark forest. Sentimental,
we swore she would never falter.

So when she started turning
into her dark sister,
we felt confused, betrayed.
More and more we heard
Tania's harder tones
usurping her soft voice.
Patty was driven underground.

She turned into Tania and we turned against her;
sooner or later the victim gets blamed.
Perhaps by then we were bored
with the innocent of the story.

So we abandoned her
in the dark forest, saying,
If you want to be Tania,
this is where you belong.

4

Stockholm Syndrome: An emotional attachment to a captor
formed as a result of conditions such as stress, dependency and
the need to cooperate for survival.
        —*Random House Unabridged Dictionary,* 2nd edition

Children never ask
why Beauty did not try to escape
when, after months or years,
the Beast unlocked the door.
They understand surrender,
how the captive, who obeys,
mutely, each detestable order,
finally decides
that the Beast is not a Beast,
but someone beautiful:
a God who could have killed her
day after day, but instead
offered her life each morning,
a daily gift. So Beauty
stopped weeping and started hoarding
his commands like tokens of love
and asked to be taught his language,
to be given a home.

5

We could not forgive Patricia
for becoming Pattania. We wanted kitsch,
the easy split into black and white,
a story in which the heroine,

bruised but pure, throws off
the Tania skin, fake fur,
a mere disguise, a sham,
the stratagem of a faithful daughter.
We could not cope with the huge
complexities of the heart,
that melting pot of selves.
And so we put her on trial,
forcing her to surrender
once more, this time to us,
the jury of her peers.

But in the end she made up
her own story. Released
from prison, she gave us the slip
by receding into the dappled
indistinct tapestry
of the common crowd
and passing into the ever-after
of the free, anonymous life.

FROM *DEPENDENCIES* (1965)

THE BLIND LEADING THE BLIND

Take my hand. There are two of us in this cave.
The sound you hear is water; you will hear it forever.
The ground you walk on is rock. I have been here before.
People come here to be born, to discover, to kiss,
to dream, and to dig and to kill. Watch for the mud.
Summer blows in with scent of horses and roses;
fall with the sound of sound breaking; winter shoves
its empty sleeve down the dark of your throat.
You will learn toads from diamonds, the fist from the palm,
love from the sweat of love, falling from flying.
There are a thousand turnoffs. I have been here before.
Once I fell off a precipice. Once I found gold.
Once I stumbled on murder, the thin parts of a girl.
Walk on, keep walking, there are axes above us.
Watch for occasional bits and bubbles of light—
birthdays for you, recognitions: *yourself, another.*
Watch for the mud. Listen for bells, for beggars.
Something with wings went crazy against my chest once.
There are two of us here. Touch me.

In the Thriving Season

In memory of my mother

Now as she catches fistfuls of sun
riding down dust and air to her crib,
my first child in her first spring
stretches bare hands back to your darkness
and heals your silence, the vast hurt
of your deaf ear and mute tongue
with doves hatched in her young throat.

Now ghost-begotten infancies
are the marrow of trees and pools
and blue uprisings in the woods
spread revolution to the mind,
I can believe birth is fathered
by death, believe that she was quick
when you forgave pain and terror
and shook the fever from your blood

Now in the thriving season of love
when the bud relents into flower,
your love turned absence has turned once more,
and if my comforts fall soft as rain
on her flutters, it is because
love grows by what it remembers of love.

The Power of Music to Disturb

A humid night. Mad June bugs dash themselves
against a window they should know is there;
I hear an owl awaking in the woods
behind our house, and wonder if it shakes
sleep from its eyes and lets its talons play,
stretch and retract, rehearsing for the kill—
and on the radio the music drives
toward death by love, for love, because of love
like some black wave that cannot break itself.

It is a music that luxuriates
in the impossibilities of love
and rides frustration till two ghosts become
alive again, aware of how the end
of every act of love is separateness;
raw, ruthless lovers, desperate enough
to bank on the absurdity of death
for royal consummation, permanence
of feeling, having, knowing, holding on.

My God, he was a devil of a man
who wrote this music so voluptuous
it sucks me in with possibilities
of sense and soul, of pity and desire
which place and time make ludicrous: I sit
across from you here in our living room
with chairs and books and red geraniums
and ordinary lamplight on the floor
after an ordinary day of love.

How can disaster be so beautiful?
I range the beaches of our lucid world
against that flood, trying to think about
our child upstairs, asleep with her light on
to keep her from vague evils; about us
whose loving has become so natural
that it has rid itself of teeth and claws,

implements for the lovers new at love,
whose jitters goad them into drawing blood.

But O my love, I cannot beat it back,
neither the sound nor what the sound lets loose;
the opulence of agony drowns out
the hard, dry smack of death against the glass
and batters down the seawalls of my mind,
and I am pulled to levels below light
where easy ways of love are meaningless
and creatures feel their way along the dark
by shock of ecstasy and heat of pain.

ON FINDING A BIRD'S
BONES IN THE WOODS

Even Einstein, gazing
at the slender ribs of the world,
examining and praising
the cool and tranquil core
under the boil and burning
of faith and metaphor—
even he, unlearning
the bag and baggage of notion,
must have kept some shred
in which to clothe that shape,
as we, who cannot escape
imagination, swaddle
this tiny world of bone
in all that we have known
of sound and motion.

CICADAS

Always in unison, they are
the rapt voice of silence,

so single-minded I cannot tell
if the sound is rich or thin,

cannot tell even if it is sound,
the high, sustained note

which gives to a summer field
involved with the sun at noon

a stillness as palpable
as smoke and mildew,

know only: when they are gone
one scrubbed autumn day

after the clean sweep
of the bright, acrid season,

what remains is a clearing of rest,
of balance and attention

but not the second skin,
hot and close, of silence.

The Mermaid

All day he had felt her stirring
under the boat, and several times
when the net had tightened, frog-nervous,
he had bungled the pulling-in,
half-glad of the stupid, open mouths
he could throw back.
                    At sundown
the shifting and holding of time and air
had brought her to the still surface,
to sun herself in the last, slow light
where lilies and leeches tangled and rocked.
He could have taken her then, aimed his net
as dragonfly hunters do when the glassy gliding
of rainbows goes to their heads,
could have carried her home on tiptoe
and lifted her lightly, ever so lightly,
over his sill.
                And, hopeless, knew
that to have her alive was only this:
the sounding, casting, waiting, seeing,
and willing the light not to move,
not yet to round the bay of her shoulder
and, passing, release her
to the darkness he would not enter.

Moon Fishing

When the moon was full they came to the water,
some with pitchforks, some with rakes,
some with sieves and ladles,
and one with a silver cup.

And they fished till a traveler passed them and said,
"Fools,
to catch the moon you must let your women
spread their hair on the water—
even the wily moon will leap to that bobbing
net of shimmering threads,
gasp and flop till its silver scales
lie black and still at your feet."

And they fished with the hair of their women
till a traveler passed them and said,
"Fools,
do you think the moon is caught lightly,
with glitter and silk threads?
You must cut out your hearts and bait your hooks
with those dark animals;
what matter you lose your hearts to reel in your dream?"

And they fished with their tight, hot hearts
till a traveler passed them and said,
"Fools,
what good is the moon to a heartless man?
Put back your hearts and get on your knees
and drink as you never have,
until your throats are coated with silver
and your voices ring like bells."

And they fished with their lips and tongues
until the water was gone
and the moon had slipped away
in the soft, bottomless mud.

A GRACKLE OBSERVED

Watching the black grackle
come out of the gray shade
into the sun, I am dazzled
by an unsuspected sheen,
yellow, purple, and green,
where the comb of light silkens
unspectacular wings—
until he, unaware
of what he means at this one
peculiar angle of sun,
hops back to his modest dark
and leaves the shining part
of himself behind, as though
brightness must outgrow
its fluttering worldly dress
and enter the mind outright
as vision, as pure light.

The Lonesome Dream

In the America of the dream
the first rise of the moon
swings free of the ocean,
and she reigns in her shining flesh
over a good, great valley
of plumed, untrampled grasses
and beasts with solemn eyes,
of lovers infallibly pitched
in their ascendant phase.

In this America, death
is virginal also, roaming
the good, great valley
in his huge boots, his shadow
steady and lean, his pistol
silver, his greeting clear
and courteous as a stranger's
who looks for another, a mind
to share his peaceable evenings.

Dreaming, we are another
race than the one which wakes
in the cold sweat of fear,
fires wild shots at death,
builds slippery towers of glass
to head him off, waylays him
with alcohol traps, rides him down
in canyons of sex, and hides
in teetering ghost towns.

Dreaming, we are the mad
who swear by the blood of trees
and speak with the tongues of streams
through props of steel and sawdust,
a colony of souls
ravaged by visions, bound
to some wild, secret cove
not yet possessed, a place
still innocent of us.

THE QUEEN OF SHEBA SAYS FAREWELL

Sir, as one royal personage to another,
let me confess that I am sick for home.
I came to test you with the hardest questions
my ministers could devise in their sessions
of finger tapping, table drumming, placing
their index fingers flat against their noses
for more incisive thought. You answered all,
spelling, besides, each complicated word
in their black dictionaries, and so gained
rights to my bed. *Noblesse oblige;* this is
proper and as it should be.

             I regret
nothing, but did not come for love—rather,
to shame you out of pride. Do you remember
how many trunks of ivory my camels
carried? One hundred elephants gave up
their eyeteeth to accommodate my need
to show you up with riches. I had hoped
to humble you with slabs of beaten gold
and openwork done by my master craftsmen,
stun you with scents of oils and precious spices,
and catch you like a brazen fly, only
to drown you in the honey of my scorn.
I failed in this, too. Solomon, I now
offer my gifts in all humility,
praising your patience.

             Still, I must go home.
Your wisdom cloys, or is beginning to;
proverbial pearls lose their luster in time.
I am uncomfortable when your scribes
doodle on their blank tablets, poised to pounce
on any utterance you care to make—
the bones you throw posterity. I long
for nervous jungle drums on these occasions,
am tempted to defy you with a dance

unseemly here. And I dislike the stare
of golden oxen in my bath; my own
taste runs to water lilies whose white faces
move with my motion.

       Let us be quite frank—
we do not suit each other, though your songs
almost persuaded me. O Solomon,
my love, my tongue of tongueless cherubim,
I shall not sleep again without your songs
deep in my ears! On long, hot evenings,
I'll teach my slaves the music of those words.
I am not a wise, just queen, not an enlightened monarch—
rather, a noble savage, quick to beat
my sad black dancers, quick to be afraid.
I fear my loneliness; I have seen lions
observe me in my hammock from the edge
of darkness after sundown. But I am sick
for my own country, where my clapping hands
command an almond tree to rise and bloom
behind my ear, and ebony girls come
and whisper to me of their love affairs.
Spring is sweeter there.

       I shall not come again.

FIGURE FOR A LANDSCAPE

Look, the solitary walker
out on this coldest Sunday of the year
shoulders the whole burden of the fable
which winter is, the moral panorama
of a silence so vast that all sounds have meaning.

In summer the landscape was simply
itself, and concealment humanly possible
in grass and shadow and the living noise
of child singers and animal dancers,
baroque in their cultivation of opulence

and the green life. But now
even the lake is petrified out of sound,
and the sky, impartially plundered
of inessential leaves, birds, clouds,
throws back his face without kindly distortion

as though he alone could answer for winter.
The tracks of the dead and the dying accost him,
crossing his footprints wherever he walks,
stands, is alive; and the clamor of ice
comes down with a crash, like an unstruck bell,

splitting his ears. In this season,
while we stay home with coffee and morning
newspapers, sensible of the danger
confronting us in the sight of a branch
gloved by a child's lost mitten,

he is the hero who bears all loss,
who, by no particular virtue
other than solitude, takes on himself
the full silence, the whole terrible
knowledge the landscape no longer conceals.

"O Brave New World, That Hath Such People in It"

Soon you will be like her, Prospero's daughter,
finding the door that leads out of yourself,
out of the rare, enameled ark of your mind,
where you live with the gracious and light-footed creatures
that thrive in the glaze of your art and freedom.

Soon you will see the face, child, of a man
with its ridges and slopes, its cisterns of natural light;
you will wander by streams across the plain of a hand,
envy the dark as it lies down on a shoulder,
and for the sake of that shoulder, that hand, that face

banish yourself from the one flawless place.

IN MEMORY OF ANTON WEBERN, DEAD SEPTEMBER 15, 1945

On leaving the house of his son-in-law in Mittersill, near Salzburg, Anton Webern, 62-year-old Austrian composer of micromusically subtilized instrumental works, is accidentally killed by an American sentinel in consequence of his failure to obey a misinterpreted signal to stop.

—Slonimsky, *Music Since 1900*

Tinged leaves lie
on the Austrian earth, like scabs
closing wounds, and guns
are stacked with last summer's hay
in warm, dry places. Home
is again a room where a crackling fire
ripens late apples on the windowsill
for a child's eventual pleasure:
so subtly does patience turn the years
and prove despair a changeling.
Women in shawls and men
with the simple minds of saints
stop at the wayside shrines
where Christ hangs dozenfold
from rusted nails, to gather
strength for the winter, as if
gathering armloads of fuel.
Yet he who coaxed
dissonant music out from behind those crude
crossings of common wood
is dead of the peace which made such intricate music
in his ears that night, is dead
of the deadly habit, is dead
of incomprehension, is dead.
May he rest easy in his fashion
of lightness, though the knuckle of our doubt
scrapes hard against his grave,
dredging his silence for the gold of purpose:
O there is hope that lambs of snow
will cover the wounded ground
with the simple charity
of whiteness one of these autumn nights,
muffling our mouths out of questions
after the sense of things.

FROM *THE PRIVATE LIFE* (1976)

Whoever You Are: A Letter

Someone who does not know you
somewhere is cleaning his rifle,
carefully weighing the bullets
that will put you out of his life.

Someone, perhaps the figure
you see in the rearview mirror,
is living ahead to your death,
dreaming the sick world green.

Someone is already climbing
a tower in Texas, is halfway up,
is at the top, has sought you out
and lifts his gun as though this death
had anything to do with you.

SMALL POEM ABOUT THE HOUNDS
AND THE HARES

After the kill, there is the feast.
And toward the end, when the dancing subsides
and the young have sneaked off somewhere,
the hounds, drunk on the blood of the hares,
begin to talk of how soft
were their pelts, how graceful their leaps,
how lovely their scared, gentle eyes.

READING THE BROTHERS
GRIMM TO JENNY

Dead means somebody has to kiss you.

Jenny, your mind commands
kingdoms of black and white:
you shoulder the crow on your left,
the snowbird on your right;
for you the cinders part
and let the lentils through,
and noise falls into place
as screech or sweet roo-coo,
while in my own, real world
gray foxes and gray wolves
bargain eye to eye,
and the amazing dove
takes shelter under the wing
of the raven to keep dry.

Knowing that you must climb,
one day, the ancient tower
where disenchantment binds
the curls of innocence,
that you must live with power
and honor circumstance,
that choice is what comes true—
O, Jenny, pure in heart,
why do I lie to you?

Why do I read you tales
in which birds speak the truth
and pity cures the blind,
and beauty reaches deep
to prove a royal mind?
Death is a small mistake
there, where the kiss revives;
Jenny, we make just dreams
out of our unjust lives.

Still, when your truthful eyes,
your keen, attentive stare,

endow the vacuous slut
with royalty, when you match
her soul to her shimmering hair,
what can she do but rise
to your imagined throne?
And what can I, but see
beyond the world that is
when, faithful, you insist
I have the golden key—
and learn from you once more
the terror and the bliss,
the world as it might be?

HIGHWAY POEMS

For Lucy and Jenny

We keep coming back and coming back
To the real: to the hotel instead of the hymns
That fall upon it out of the wind
                  —Wallace Stevens, "An Ordinary Evening
                                    in New Haven"

1

The narrow black veins on the map
will get you there, but the fat
red arteries get you there quicker
and without pain:
you can go from the head
to the toes of America
without seeing
a hospital or a jail,
without ever coming on tears
                  toys
                  wrinkles
                  scars
                  fists
                  guns
                  crossed fingers
                  broken teeth

2

Between the roof of the Howard Johnson
and the star of the Holiday Inn
falls the shadow
which is myself.

Question: am I real
when I exist only
inside a hot steel body
at seventy miles per hour
and when I'm freed, become
a certain car-door slam,
a brief pattern of footsteps
outside a numbered door?

3

Hardly anyone takes
the old state road anymore.
The town is dying,
its blood being pumped
into the new expressway
five miles east of here.
Sad and miraculous now,
transfigured by extinction,
are the ones who stay
to go down with the town:
the proprietor of the General Store
and the Restwell Cabins (vacancy always)
and the postmistress, his wife,
angel of government checks
and news from a world with receding walls.

4

Camping, you learn people
by their shoes in the toilet stalls.
The brown loafers support
white legs and a silver trailer;
the navy tennis shoes go
with Pepsodent and a black wig;
the tiny saddle shoes match a voice
that talks about being three;
and I must be a pair
of yellow sneakers, blue-patched at the toes,
although, being filled with my life,
I don't believe it.

5   ILLINOIS, INDIANA, IOWA

Austrian food is not served in Vienna,
and people in Paris drink Coke, not wine.
Lebanon has its Little League
and Warsaw its Civil War cannon.
Carthage is full of blondes,
and Cairo divides, American-style,
into white and black, money and rage.
Gnawbone keeps teasing, a tricky riddle,

and What Cheer defies punctuation,
but Stony Lonesome is all that it says.
I have seen Hindustan—Hoosier twang,
no belly dancing allowed—
and I have been in Arcadia:
one street by a railroad track,
blue chicory, goldenrod.

O telltale country, fact and mirage,
coat of many colors
stitched in homesickness, threaded with dreams,
land of seven fat cows,
is it finished, your poem?

6

We keep coming back to the old hotel,
to the old Main Street, in the old part of town,
to the tottering giant, the elephant
sagging on concrete feet.

We keep coming back to the white-railed porch,
the geraniums and the wicker chairs,
the glass doors and the Persian carpet,
the banquet hall with the chandeliers
where the Chamber of Commerce meets and talks
about pride and achievement, while the stores
on the block are vacant, their windows blind,
their clerks gone to the big new mall
outside of town, where the chain stores are
with check-out lanes and shopping carts,
where shoplifting is a crime.

We keep coming back to the corpses of elms
imagining shade, umbrellas of peace,
imagining grandparents, newspapers, cups,
people out walking, the ticket booth
of the movie theater occupied—
were times really better when the hotel
served the best Sunday dinner around
and the bridal suite was booked solid,
when the governor campaigned on the steps,
promising dollars for votes?

We keep coming back to what we gave up;
remember, we never wanted to live here
in the days of parades and the Firemen's Ball
and the high-school musical once a year.
No, these are deathbed visits: regrets,
surprising grief and sudden love,
terror of loss, the need to lay
hands on the past before it is gone,
hold on to the knowledge at least, if not
the stairs and walls of our history,
walk away weeping at least, assured
that sometime, a long time ago,
we came from somewhere, that we are real.

THE FALL OF THE MUSE

Her wings are sold for scrap,
her tiara goes to the museum.
She takes off her purple gown,
her long gloves.
In her underwear she is anyone.

Even when she is naked, they laugh.
It's not enough, they shout.
Take off your pubic hair,
mutilate your breasts,
cut off a finger,
put a patch on your left eye.

Now she is one of us.
She laughs the small laugh of the ordinary.
She gives us all equal kisses.
She counts her money at inaugural balls.
She is searched at airports.
She depends on sleeping pills.
She betrays art with life.
She lectures on the catharsis of drivel.
She learns about Mount Olympus from quiz shows.

She moves in a circle of victims;
they make her eat her heart in public.
She has been bled so many times
her blood has lost its color.
She comes on the stage on all fours
but insists that her teeth be straightened.

Democratic, she sits with us.
We share the flat bread of affluence,
the suicidal water;
we kill each other with jokes.
She wears false eyelashes
when she throws herself off the bridge.

THE BIOGRAPHER

A biography is something one invents.
        —Louis Ferdinand Céline

God knows I've used
what surgical skills I have
to open you up through minor incisions—
larger ones might not have healed,
left you a cripple or a corpse,
and I love you too much for that.

For years, I lived
on a diet of your words,
letters, diaries, the collected works,
till they dropped from my mouth like pits
each time I spoke, and my friends
could smell you on my breath.

I took the journeys you took,
walked in your tracks like a Chinese wife;
asleep, I spoke in your dreams.
I would have eaten your heart;
like Snow White's mother I wanted to turn into you,
but chaste and tricky, you slipped through your facts.

I came to live in your house,
restored your pictures, bought back your books,
discovered the key to your desk,
moved the yellow chair to the window—
and now you come in, asking
whose house this is.

January Afternoon, with Billie Holiday

For Studs Terkel

Her voice shifts as if it were light,
from chalk to parchment to oil.
I think of the sun this morning,
how many knives were flashed
through black, compliant trees;
now she has aged it with her singing,
turned it to milk thinned with water,
a poor people's sun, enough
knowledge to go around.

I want to dance, to bend
as gradually as a flower,
release a ball in slow motion
to follow in the marvelous path
of an unfolding jet streak,
love's expansive finger
across the cheek of the sky,
"Heaven, I'm in heaven . . ."

The foolish old songs were right,
the heart does, actually, ache
from trying to push beyond
itself, this room, the world,
all that can be imagined;
space is not enough space
for its sudden immensity . . .

I am not what you think
This is not what I wanted

Desire has no object, it simply happens,
rises and floats, lighter than air—
but she knows that. Her voice scrapes
against the innocent words of the song;
tomorrow is something she remembers.

LIFE OF A QUEEN

1 CHILDHOOD

For two days her lineage is in doubt,
then someone deciphers the secret message.
They build a pendulous chamber
for her, and stuff her with sweets.

Workers keep bringing her royal jelly.
She knows nothing of other lives,
about digging in purple crocus
and round dances in the sun.

Poor and frail little rich girl,
she grows immense in her hothouse.
Whenever she tries to stop eating,
they open her mouth and force it down.

2 THE FLIGHT

She marries him in midair;
    for a moment
he is ennobled, a prince.

She gives the signal
    for their embrace;
over too soon. O, nevermore.

Bruised, she drags herself from
    his dead body,
finds her way back exhausted.

She is bathed, curtains are drawn.
    Ten thousand lives
settle inside her belly.

Now to the only labor she knows.
    She remembers
nothing of him, or their fall.

3   THE RECLUSE

They make it plain
her term is over.
No one comes;
they let her starve.

The masses, her children,
whip up sweets
for a young beauty
who is getting fat.

Nothing to do.
Her ovaries paper,
her sperm sac dust,
she shrivels away.

A crew disassembles
her royal cell.
Outside, a nation
crowns its queen.

ALIVE TOGETHER

Speaking of marvels, I am alive
together with you, when I might have been
alive with anyone under the sun,
when I might have been Abélard's woman
or the whore of a Renaissance pope
or a peasant wife with not enough food
and not enough love, with my children
dead of the plague. I might have slept
in an alcove next to the man
with the golden nose, who poked it
into the business of stars,
or sewn a starry flag
for a general with wooden teeth.
I might have been the exemplary Pocahontas
or a woman without a name
weeping in Master's bed
for my husband, exchanged for a mule,
my daughter, lost in a drunken bet.
I might have been stretched on a totem pole
to appease a vindictive god
or left, a useless girl-child,
to die on a cliff. I like to think
I might have been Mary Shelley
in love with a wrongheaded angel,
or Mary's friend. I might have been you.
This poem is endless, the odds against us are endless,
our chances of being alive together
statistically nonexistent;
still we have made it, alive in a time
when rationalists in square hats
and hatless Jehovah's Witnesses
agree it is almost over,
alive with our lively children
who—but for endless ifs—
might have missed out on being alive
together with marvels and follies
and longings and lies and wishes

and error and humor and mercy
and journeys and voices and faces
and colors and summers and mornings
and knowledge and tears and chance.

My Grandmother's Gold Pin

The first fleur-de-lis is for green-stemmed glasses with swirls,
which were called Romans / for the cow with the brown fleece,
which said moo when we bent its neck / for the elegant braids
on my grandfather's shabby jacket; my grandfather who was
poor and proud and loving:

The second is for the upright on which my aunt played Schubert
impromptus (though we shivered with joy at "Rustles of Spring") /
for the cactus which bumped the ceiling / for the silk and
ebony fans that clicked into bloom in my grandmother's cold
bedroom / for the same dark dress she wore every day, making
her bosom cozy under her round smile / for snowdrops with
modestly lowered heads, which we bought at the corner for
every one of her birthdays, rushing spring by two days:

The third is for cherry soup, beer soup, and chocolate soup,
served in thin china bowls with gold edges / for my grandfather's
walking stick with its silver head swinging, when we walked
past red rhododendrons and ponds full of hand-fed swans / for
the hours of pachisi / for red, lustrous dominoes, heavy as
gems in the hand / for the card tricks up my grandfather's
sleeve; merry secrets of one who was totally deaf, who was
gentle and gay and a child among children:

The fourth is for a white china hen with fresh eggs in her
belly / for darning days, when my grandmother traded us
mended socks for crisp brown flounder / for my grandfather's
treasure of butterflies / for Roman candles, his credible
galaxies / for the red leather albums of postage stamps, precious
untouchables which went, one by one, for the roof over their
heads:

And the pearl in the center is for remembrance / for never
forgetting the war, flight, madness, and hunger which killed
them / for never forgiving that death in an animal shed /
for the flowers I'd bring, if I could, to the grave on the
other side of a Wall which should be a metaphor or a bad dream /

and for the passion of sorrow, senseless and pure, which is
all I can give in return to them, who were truly good:

And that, my daughter, is why I wear it / and because it is
all I have left of an age when people believed the heart was
an organ of goodness, and light was stronger than darkness,
that death came to you in your proper time—
an age when the dream of Man nearly came true.

ON READING AN
ANTHOLOGY OF POSTWAR
GERMAN POETRY

America saved me
and history played me false:
I was not crushed
under rubble, nor was I beaten
along a frozen highway;
my children are not dead
of postwar hunger;
my love is back, with his brain
intact, his toes accounted for;
I have forced no one
into the chamber of death.

My habits have not been broken.
For me, rock
stands for dignity, fire
is an element, the moon
is not necessarily poisoned,
snow exists for its own sake.

I know enough to refuse to say
that life is good,
but I act as though it were,
and skeptical about love, I survive
by the witness of my own.

*

I am among these poets
a Briar Rose, a Rip Van Winkle,
a stranger to their courage
as they raise a new language
out of wreckage and evil
and terrible knowledge. I marvel
as the newborn Word
lifts itself from the ruins
and splits, a living cell,
into its destinies.

What the Dog Perhaps Hears

If an inaudible whistle
blown between our lips
can send him home to us,
then silence is perhaps
the sound of spiders breathing
and roots mining the earth;
it may be asparagus heaving,
headfirst, into the light
and the long brown sound
of cracked cups, when it happens.
We would like to ask the dog
if there is a continuous whir
because the child in the house
keeps growing, if the snake
really stretches full length
without a click and the sun
breaks through clouds without
a decibel of effort,
whether in autumn, when the trees
dry up their wells, there isn't a shudder
too high for us to hear.

What is it like up there
above the shut-off level
of our simple ears?
For us there was no birth cry,
the newborn bird is suddenly here,
the egg broken, the nest alive,
and we heard nothing when the world changed.

PALINDROME

There is less difficulty—indeed, no logical difficulty at all—in imagining two portions of the universe, say two galaxies, in which time goes one way in one galaxy and the opposite way in the other. . . . Intelligent beings in each galaxy would regard their own time as "forward" and time in the other galaxy as "backward."

—Martin Gardner, in *Scientific American*

Somewhere now she takes off the dress I am
putting on. It is evening in the antiworld
where she lives. She is forty-five years away
from her death, the hole which spit her out
into pain, impossible at first, later easing,
going, gone. She has unlearned much by now.
Her skin is firming, her memory sharpens,
her hair has grown glossy. She sees without glasses,
she falls in love easily. Her husband has lost his
shuffle, they laugh together. Their money shrinks,
but their ardor increases. Soon her second child
will be young enough to fight its way into her
body and change its life to monkey to frog to
tadpole to cluster of cells to tiny island to
nothing. She is making a list:
>   *Things I will need in the past*
>   lipstick
>   shampoo
>   transistor radio
>   Sergeant Pepper
>   acne cream
>   five-year diary with a lock

She is eager, having heard about adolescent love
and the freedom of children. She wants to read
Crime and Punishment and ride on a roller coaster
without getting sick. I think of her as she will
be at fifteen, awkward, too serious. In the
mirror I see she uses her left hand to write,
her other to open a jar. By now our lives should
have crossed. Somewhere sometime we must have
passed one another like going and coming trains,
with both of us looking the other way.

Snow

Telephone poles relax their spines;
sidewalks go under. The nightly groans
of aging porches are put to sleep.
Mercy sponges the lips of stairs.

While we talk in the old concepts—
time that was, and things that are—
snow has leveled the stumps of the past
and the earth has a new language.

It is like the scene in which the girl
moves toward the hero
who has not yet said, "Come here."

Come here, then. Every ditch
has been exalted. We are covered with stars.
Feel how light they are, our lives.

The Private Life

What happens, happens in silence:

the man from New York City
feels himself going insane
and flies to Brazil to rest,

the piano student in Indiana
lovingly gathers the prune pits
Horowitz left on his plate
the only time he ate breakfast there,

my daughter daydreams of marriage,
she has suddenly grown
three inches taller than I,

and now, this icy morning,
we find another tree,
an aspen, doubled over,
split in two at the waist:
no message, no suicide note.

*

Fruit market:
age-spotted avocados,
lemons with gooseflesh;
navel oranges,
pears with flushed cheeks;
apples like buttocks,
pineapples like stockades,
coconut heads with instructions:
"Pierce the eyes with an awl,
allowing the milk to run out,
then tap hard with a hammer
until the outer covering cracks . . ."

Life, our violent history,
lies speechless and mild in these bins.

We are being eaten by words.
My face is smeared with headlines.
My lungs, blue tubes, are always on.
You come home smelling of printer's ink.

The teletype is a dragon's mouth;
ripped out, its tongue grows back
at the speed of sound:

Five thousand tons of explosives were dropped
The terrorist wore a business suit
His late-model Triumph was found overturned
She said she had taken fertility drugs
The boy stood on the burning deck
The girl's body was found in a cornfield
The President joked with newsmen
The two youths were killed execution-style
The National Safety Council reported
A spokesman for the hospital said
The blond actress disclosed

YOUR HOUSE IS ON FIRE, YOUR CHILDREN ARE GONE

Stop it. What happens,
happens in silence:
in a red blood cell,
a curl in the brain,
in the ignorant ovum,
the switched-on nerves;

it happens in eyes before the scream,
in memory when it boils over,
in the ravine of conscience,
in the smile that says, *Come to bed.*

Today—my snowcapped birthday—
our red hibiscus is blooming again.
Months of refusal; now
one sudden silent flower,
one inscrutable life.

THE LATE NEWS

For months, numbness
in the face of broadcasts;
I stick to my resolution
not to bleed
when my blood helps no one.

For months, I accept
my smooth skin,
my gratuitous life as my due;
then suddenly, a crack—
the truth seeps through like acid,
a child without eyes to weep with
weeps for me, and I bleed
as if I were still human.

A NUDE BY
EDWARD HOPPER

For Margaret Gaul

The light
drains me of what I might be,
a man's dream
of heat and softness;
or a painter's—
breasts cozy pigeons,
arms gently curved
by a temperate noon.

I am
blue veins, a scar,
a patch of lavender cells,
used thighs and shoulders;
my calves
are as scant as my cheeks,
my hips won't plump
small, shimmering pillows:

but this body
is home, my childhood
is buried here, my sleep
rises and sets inside,
desire
crested and wore itself thin
between these bones—
I live here.

In Praise of Surfaces

When I touch you
with hands or mouth,
I bless your skin,
the sweet rind
through which you breathe,
the only part
I can possess. Even
that branch of you
which moves inside me
does not deliver your soul:
one flesh is all
the mystery we were promised.

2

"To learn about the invisible,
look at the visible," says
the Talmud. I have seen you
for so long you are
ground into the walls,
so long I can't remember
your face when you're away,
so long I have to look
each night when you come home
at the tall surprise you bring
me, time and time again.

3

Words too are surfaces
scraped or shaken loose.
When I listen to you
I pick up rocks,
shells, algae
brought up from darkness.

Sometimes I
come close to catching
a fish bare-handed;
angling, I always fail.
No skin diver, I
could never reach bottom;
rock by wet rock,
piecemeal,
I collect you.

NAMING THE ANIMALS

Until he named the horse
                horse,
hoofs left no print on the earth,
manes had not been invented,
swiftness and grace were not married.

Until he named the cow
                cow,
no one slept standing up,
no one saw through opaque eyes,
food was chewed only once.

Only after he named the fish
                fish,
did the light put on skins
of yellow and silver oil,
revealing itself as a dancer
and high-jump champion of the world,

just as later
he had to name the woman
                love
before he could put on the knowledge
of who she was, with her small hands.

Love like Salt

It lies in our hands in crystals
too intricate to decipher

It goes into the skillet
without being given a thought

It spills on the floor, so fine
we step all over it

We carry a pinch behind each eyeball

It breaks out on our foreheads

We store it inside our bodies
in secret wineskins

At supper, we pass it around the table
talking of holidays by the sea

The Concert

In memory of Dimitri Mitropoulos

The harpist believes there is music
in the skeletons of fish

The French horn player believes
in enormous golden snails

The piano believes in nothing
and grins from ear to ear

Strings are scratching their bellies
openly, enjoying it

Flutes and oboes complain
in dialects of the same tongue

Drumsticks rattle a calfskin
from the sleep of another life

because the supernatural crow
on the podium flaps his wings
and death is no excuse

A Farewell, a Welcome

After the lunar landings

Good-bye pale cold inconstant
tease, you never existed
therefore we had to invent you

    Good-bye crooked little man
    huntress who sleeps alone
    dear pastor, shepherd of stars
    who tucked us in   Good-bye

Good riddance phony prop
con man moon
who tap-danced with June
to the tender surrender
of love from above

Good-bye decanter of magic liquids
fortuneteller *par excellence*
seducer   incubus   medicine man
exile's sanity   love's sealed lips
womb that nourished the monstrous child
and the sweet ripe grain   Good-bye
    We trade you in as we traded
    the evil eye for the virus
    the rosy seat of affections
    for the indispensable pump
we say good-bye as we said good-bye
to angels in nightgowns   to Grandfather God

Good-bye forever Edam and Gorgonzola
cantaloupe in the sky
night watchman, one-eyed loner
wolves nevertheless
are programed to howl   Good-bye
    forbidden lover good-bye
    sleepwalkers will wander
    with outstretched arms for no reason
    while you continue routinely

to husband the sea, prevail
in the fix of infant strabismus
Good-bye ripe ovum women will spill their blood
in spite of you now lunatics wave good-bye
accepting despair by another name

Welcome new world to the brave old words
Peace Hope Justice
Truth Everlasting welcome
ash-colored playground of children
happy in airy bags
never to touch is never to miss it

Scarface hello we've got you covered
welcome untouchable outlaw
with an alias in every country
salvos and roses you are home
our footprints stamp you mortal

HOPE

It hovers in dark corners
before the lights are turned on,
  it shakes sleep from its eyes
  and drops from mushroom gills,
    it explodes in the starry heads
    of dandelions turned sages,
      it sticks to the wings of green angels
      that sail from the tops of maples.

It sprouts in each occluded eye
of the many-eyed potato,
  it lives in each earthworm segment
  surviving cruelty,
    it is the motion that runs
    from the eyes to the tail of a dog,
      it is the mouth that inflates the lungs
      of the child that has just been born.

It is the singular gift
we cannot destroy in ourselves,
the argument that refutes death,
the genius that invents the future,
all we know of God.

It is the serum which makes us swear
not to betray one another;
it is in this poem, trying to speak.

LETTER FROM THE END
OF THE WORLD

The reason no longer matters,
the lamp, my curiosity,
my sisters' insinuations,
never waking up together,
you saying, "Trust me."

The point is the end of innocence
comes when you look at someone you love
asleep and see how his eyeballs flicker
under their shallow lids.

The point is since I lost you
I have been going around the world
looking for you and finding myself
instead, small scraps of a woman
that are beginning to fit.

At first the mountains closed ranks against me,
blackberries dried in my mouth,
the wind kept turning to face me.
Wherever I came, the music stopped,
sidewalks opened up manholes,
lights went out,
a pregnant woman shielded her face.

But I learned to sleep on the ground
despite the heartbeat of giant oaks
and the moon's soft taunts at the sun,
the all-night labor of heaving roots,
the mushroom smell of death.

I learned not to throw the bouquets
the wretched made of their wounds
back in their faces, to accept
tears brought me on red pillows,
to knock on plain white doors
without windows or peepholes, not knowing
whose voice would say, "Come in."

The point is I came back
from the deep places. Always
there was help, a man or woman
who asked no questions, an animal's
warm body, the itch in my muscles
to climb a swinging rope.

I started out as a girl
without a shadow, in iron shoes;
now, at the end of the world
I am a woman full of rain.
The journey back should be easy;
if this reaches you, wait for me.

FROM *THE NEED TO HOLD STILL* (1980)

For a Thirteenth Birthday

You have read *War and Peace.*
Now here is *Sister Carrie,*
not up to Tolstoy; still
it will second the real world:
predictable planes and levels,
pavement that holds you,
stairs that lift you,
ice that trips you,
nights that begin after sunset,
four lunar phases,
a finite house.

I give you Dreiser
although (or because)
I am no longer sure.
Lately I have been walking into glass doors.
Through the car windows, curbs disappear.
On the highway, wrong turnoffs become irresistible,
someone else is controlling the wheel.
Sleepless nights pile up like a police record;
all my friends are getting divorced.
Language, my old comrade, deserts me;
words are misused or forgotten,
consonants fight each other
between my upper and lower teeth.
I write *fiend* for *friend*
and *word* for *world,*
remember comes out with an *m* missing.

I used to be able to find my way in the dark,
sure of the furniture,
but the town I lived in for years
has pulled up its streets in my absence,
disguised its buildings behind my back.
My neighbor at dinner glances
at his cuffs, his palms;
he has memorized certain phrases,

but does not speak my language.
Suddenly I am aware
no one at the table does.

And so I give you Dreiser,
his measure of certainty:
a table that's oak all the way through,
real and fragrant flowers,
skirts from sheep and silkworms,
no unknown fibers;
a language as plain as money,
a workable means of exchange;
a world whose very meanness is solid,
mud into mortar, and you are sure
of what will injure you.

I give you names like nails,
walls that withstand your pounding,
doors that are hard to open,
but once they are open, admit you
into rooms that breathe pure sun.
I give you trees that lose their leaves,
as you knew they would,
and then come green again.
I give you
fruit preceded by flowers,
Venus supreme in the sky,
the miracle of always
landing on your feet,
even though the earth
rotates on its axis.

Start out with that, at least.

ANOTHER VERSION

Our trees are aspens, but people
mistake them for birches;
they think of us as characters
in a Russian novel, Kitty and Levin
living contentedly in the country.
Our friends from the city watch the birds
and rabbits feeding together
on top of the deep, white snow.
(We have Russian winters in Illinois,
but no sleigh bells, possums instead of wolves,
no trusted servants to do our work.)
As in a Russian play, an old man
lives in our house, he is my father;
he lets go of life in such slow motion,
year after year, that the grief
is stuck inside me, a poisoned apple
that won't go up or down.
But like the three sisters, we rarely speak
of what keeps us awake at night;
like them, we complain about things
that don't really matter and talk
of our pleasures and of the future:
we tell each other the willows
are early this year, hazy with green.

DRAWINGS BY CHILDREN

1

The sun may be visible or not
(it may be behind you,
the viewer of these pictures)
but the sky is always blue
if it is day. If not,
the stars come almost within your grasp;
crooked, they reach out to you,
on the verge of falling.
It is never sunrise or sunset;
there is no bloody eye
spying on you across the horizon.
It is clearly day or night,
it is bright or totally dark,
it is here and never there.

2

In the beginning, you only needed
your head, a moon swimming in space,
and four bare branches;
and when your body was added,
it was light and thin at first,
not yet the dark chapel
from which, later, you tried to escape.
You lived in a non-Newtonian world,
your arms grew up from your shoulders,
your feet did not touch the ground,
your hair was streaming,
you were still flying.

3

The house is smaller than you remembered,
it has windows but no door.
A chimney sits on the gable roof,

a curl of smoke reassures you.
But the house has only two dimensions,
like a mask without its face;
the people who live there stand outside
as though time were always summer—
there is nothing behind the wall
except a space where the wind whistles,
but you cannot see that.

FICTION

Going south, we watched spring
unroll like a proper novel:
forsythia, dogwood, rose;
bare trees, green lace, full shade.
By the time we arrived in Georgia
the complications were deep.

When we drove back, we read
from back to front. Maroon went wild,
went scarlet, burned once more
and then withdrew into pink,
tentative, still in bud.
I thought if only we could go on
and meet again, shy as strangers.

Sometimes, When the Light

Sometimes, when the light strikes at odd angles
and pulls you back into childhood

and you are passing a crumbling mansion
completely hidden behind old willows

or an empty convent guarded by hemlocks
and giant firs standing hip to hip,

you know again that behind that wall,
under the uncut hair of the willows

something secret is going on,
so marvelous and dangerous

that if you crawled through and saw,
you would die, or be happy forever.

Beginning with 1914

Since it always begins
in the unlikeliest place,
we start in an obsolete country
on no current map. The camera
glides over flower beds,
for this is a southern climate.
We focus on medals, a horse,
on a white uniform,
for this is June. The young man
waves to the people lining the road,
he lifts a child, he catches
a rose from a wrinkled woman
in a blue kerchief. Then we hear shots
and close in on a casket
draped in the Austrian flag.
Thirty-one days torn off a calendar.
Bombs on Belgrade; then Europe explodes.
We watch the trenches fill with men,
the air with live ammunition.
A close-up of a five-year-old
living on turnips. Her older sister,
my not-yet-mother, already
wearing my daughter's eyes,
is reading a letter as we cut
to a young man with thick glasses
who lies in a trench and writes
a study of Ibsen. I recognize him,
he is going to be my father,
and this is his way of keeping alive.
Snow. Blood. Lice. Frostbite.
Grenades. Stretchers. Coffins. Snow.
Telegrams with black borders.
On the wide screen my father returns
bringing his brother's body;
my mother's father brings back his son's
from the opposite edge. They come together
under the oaks of the cemetery.

All who will be my family
are here, except my sister,
who is not yet imagined.
Neither am I, who imagine
this picture, who now jump
to my snowy birthday in the year
of the million-mark loaf of bread.
My early years are played
by a blue-eyed child who grows up
quickly, for this is a film
of highlights, like all documentaries
false to the life—the work
of selective memory, all I can bear
of a painful childhood. The swastika
appears and remains as the huge
backdrop against which we're seen.
The sound track of a hysterical voice
is threatening us. We're heard as whispers.
Shortly before my city
bursts into flames, my stand-in
disappears from the film, which continues
with scenes of terror and death
I can't bear to watch. I pick up
a new reel, a strange sequel
set in a different location
and made in another language,
in which I am back. The colors are bright,
the sound track is filled with music,
the focus gentle. A man is beside me.
Time-lapse photography picks up
the inchmeal growth of daughters
toward the sky, the slow subversion
of dark by gray hair. Little happens.
The camera sums up the even flow
of many years in a shot of a river.
The principals from part one
are missing, except for me
who am the connection. The time is now,
and I am playing myself.

TALKING TO HELEN
Helen Keller, 1880–1968

1   THE SOURCE

A well
that ran deeper
than roots
and memory

a spring
that wanted to climb
into a world
of mirrors

a pump and a hand
that spoke
the thing and its name

the flash
so cold, so clear
it burned like ice
before
it bloomed
into light

2   THE WORD *WATER*

The word *water,* meaning

what leaps on your hands
under the pump

what crawls down your back
from the washcloth

what runs down your cheeks
and tastes salty

what licks your feet
in the early morning grass

what spits out smooth rocks
and lets you fly like a fish

what coaxes green
from black and brown seeds
(Helen, try to imagine green!)

what has one home in the sky,
another in the earth

what will teach you
the word *deep*
and the word *cleanse*

the word *flow*
and the word *drown*

the word *inexhaustible*
and the word *birth*

what is beginning to quench your thirst
for the real name of the world

3   THE SAVIORS

Before you knew the word *dream*
and the word *fire,* you dreamed of fires.
Later you wrote how the swaying shapes—
orange, were they, did you
dream in color?—
closed in around you, hot
and threatening, a lynch mob
from which you could not escape
except by screaming and waking.
Then the words came,
kept coming: *water, mother,*
father, flower, door,
earth, give, open,
a growing army, proof
against the ring of fire.
You slept. You smiled in your sleep.
You slept all night without screaming.
You still did not know the word
language, the word *saved.*

4 THE WORD *FEELING*

"You feel with your fingers,"
the teacher told us,
dismissing expressions
of love and fear.
He was a tyrant
and wore a large ring.

Years later, I understood,
when I read about you, at twelve,
in a Niagara Falls hotel,
your face overwhelmed
by the roar you felt
when you pressed your fingers
against the windowsill,

and how, on another day,
you said you loved white roses,
meaning the thin-skinned sisters
of the fleshier reds.

5 THE WORD *VAST*

Flying above the clouds
I am in a blank space,
perhaps a sunlit version
of your darker world.

And breaking through the clouds
I am above a country
scaled to your palpable map,
your raised geography.

I dream of touching the winter trees,
their stiff unruly hair,
and the collection of roofs
from a child's bag of blocks;
the land laid out like a chocolate bar,
squares bordered by ridges
that intersect at right angles;
hills that fit in the palm of your hand,
railroad tracks for your fingers.

I used to wonder how you made
the leap from your shallow liquid
to the real Mississippi,
how you got to the ships that lie
on the Atlantic floor.

But coming down, approaching—
wheels out, already gripping
the runway—I think it was easy.
Your world was imagination,
all possible worlds, while mine
shrinks with the speed of speed.

One hour: New York/Chicago.
The long drawn-out idea
of the word *vast* contracts
into four brief letters,
already obsolete.

6 THE WORD *AUTUMN*

Helen, this is a maple leaf.
It is a hand. Put your fingers
against the five of the leaf
and feel how they match.
It is golden,
that is to say the feeling
that lies down deep inside you
like an unhurried animal
and keeps you warm longer
than green or red. Each tree
has a thousand golden hands,
soon they will fall around you.
Helen, it is autumn,
the sun today bears down
intense as an evangelist
and imprints each hand once more
with its large signature
before moving on to another town.

DAUGHTER

My next poem will be happy,
I promise myself. Then you come
with your deep eyes, your tall jeans,
your narrow hands, your wit,
your uncanny knowledge, and
your loneliness. All the flowers
your father planted, all
the green beans that have made it,
all the world's recorded pianos
and this exhilarating day
cannot change that.

MERCE CUNNINGHAM AND THE BIRDS

Last night I saw Merce Cunningham and his ten amazing dancers
dancing for eighty minutes without a break in the college gym.

I am trying to tell you how it was
        but of course there are no words
        for being wholly enclosed in a space,
        a tight cocoon without chinks
        so none of the wonder will leak out

Instead, I ask you to watch the assorted birds
feeding outside this window,
darting and dropping and zeroing in,
assuming positions in groups of threes
        or fours, to break up and form
        new patterns, other groups

how each incessant performer
signals a personal flash of color:
cardinal red, jay blue,
towhee orange, March pea green
        of not-yet-yellow goldfinch,
always tempered with black

how even their silences prefigure
shifts already known to the muscles

        and how none leads or follows
        how each moves
        to the authority of its brain
        its autonomous body

        perpetual proof that the world

is energy, that to land
in a certain space at a certain time
is being alive; watch how they manage
to keep it up till each soul is fed

        and disappear into nowhere

NOT ONLY THE ESKIMOS

We have only one noun
but as many different kinds:

the grainy snow of the Puritans
and snow of soft, fat flakes,

guerrilla snow, which comes in the night
and changes the world by morning,

rabbinical snow, a permanent skullcap
on the highest mountains,

snow that blows in like the Lone Ranger,
riding hard from out of the West,

surreal snow in the Dakotas,
when you can't find your house, your street,
though you are not in a dream
or a science-fiction movie,

snow that tastes good to the sun
when it licks black tree limbs,
leaving us only one white stripe,
a replica of a skunk,

unbelievable snows:
the blizzard that strikes on the tenth of April,
the false snow before Indian summer,
the Big Snow on Mozart's birthday,
when Chicago became the Elysian Fields
and strangers spoke to each other,

paper snow, cut and taped
to the inside of grade-school windows,

in an old tale, the snow
that covers a nest of strawberries,
small hearts, ripe and sweet,

the special snow that goes with Christmas,
whether it falls or not,

the Russian snow we remember
along with the warmth and smell of our furs,
though we have never traveled
to Russia or worn furs,

Villon's snows of yesteryear,
lost with ladies gone out like matches,
the snow in Joyce's "The Dead,"
the silent, secret snow
in a story by Conrad Aiken,
which is the snow of first love,

the snowfall between the child
and the spacewoman on TV,

snow as idea of whiteness,
as in *snowdrop, snow goose, snowball bush,*

the snow that puts stars in your hair,
and your hair, which has turned to snow,

the snow Elinor Wylie walked in
in velvet shoes,

the snow before her footprints
and the snow after,

the snow in the back of our heads,
whiter than white, which has to do
with childhood again each year.

FOUND IN
THE CABBAGE PATCH

The shiny head is round,
full term, between
the spread leaves of its mother.
I come as the midwife,
a kitchen knife in my hand.

There. No lusty cry,
this child is silent.
Two white moths
hover and flutter,
milky attendants
in perpetual motion.

I leave the mother's wound
for the sun to heal.
The stump of the newborn
dries in the crook of my arm.
I am the witch, cradling
the pale green head,
murmuring, "Little one,
you look good enough to eat."

ONE MORE HYMN TO THE SUN

You know that like an ideal mother
she will never leave you,
though after a week of rain
you begin to worry

but you accept her brief absences,
her occasional closed doors
as the prerogative
of an eccentric lover

You know which side of the bed
she gets up on,
though, being a night person,
you are on more intimate terms
with the moon, who lets you watch,
while the sun will put out your eyes
for tampering with her privacy

She wants to be known by her parts,
fingers, a flashing leg,
a cheek, a shoulder; by things
spilled from her purse:
small change, a patterned scarf,
mirrors, keys, an earring

You like the fact that her moods
are an orderly version of yours,
arranged, like the needs of animals,
by seasons: her spring quirks,
her sexual summers,
her steadfast warmth in the fall;
you remember her face on Christmas Day,
blurred, and suffused with the weak smile
of a woman who has just given birth

The way she loves you, your whole body,
and still leaves enough space between you

to keep you from turning to cinders
before your time!

You admit she colors
everything you see,
that Renoir and Monet
are her direct descendants;
she could make you say
the grass is red, the snow purple

She never gave up on you
though it took you billions of years
to learn the alphabet
and the shadow you cast on the ground
changed its shape again and again

THE COOK
After Vermeer

1

No wonder she thinks there's more
where everything came from

a girl as round as the jug
that never runs dry

her arms thick cream, her yellow bodice
filled with anticipation

the bread before her risen
in the same light in which she stands

2

She did not ask for this,
three centuries of tilting
a half-filled glazed brown jug
to show us the connection

the give-and-take, the earthen lip
feeding the earthen bowl

herself still bound to us
who watch the milk: it pours
and keeps on pouring,
although the paint is dry

PICKING RASPBERRIES

Once the thicket opens
and lets you enter
and the first berry dissolves on your tongue,

you will remember nothing
of your old life. You can stay
in that country of sun and silence
as long as you like. To return,

you have only to look at your arms
and discover the long, red marks.
You will have invented pain,
which has no place there.

THE NEED TO
HOLD STILL

Winter weeds,
survivors
of a golden age,
take over the open land,
pale armies
redressing the balance

Again we live ·
in a time of fasting,
burlap cassocks,
monks on their knees,
bells tolling
in an empty sky

among the thin,
the trampled-on,
the inarticulate
clothed in drafts
and rooted in shocked earth
which remembers nothing

fields and fields of them

*

Teasel
yarrow
goldenrod
wheat
bedstraw
Queen Anne's lace
drop-seed
love grass:
plain, strong names,
bread and water

A woman
coming in from a walk

notices how drab
her hair has become
that gray and brown
are colors
she disappears into

that her body
has stopped asking
for anything except calm

*

When she brings them
into the house
and shortens them
for the vase,
their stems break
like old bones,
clean

No holding on
No bitter odor
No last drop of juice

Hers, as long as she wants them

Their freedom from either/or
will outlast hers every time

*

The dignity of form
after seduction
and betrayal
by color

the heads,
separate,
but held together
by an old design
no one has thought
to question

the open pods
that have given
and given again

dullness of straw,
which underlies
the rose
the grape
the kiss

the narrow leaf blades,
shape of the body

the fine stems,
earliest brushstrokes,
lines in the rock
on the wall
the page

VOICES FROM THE FOREST

1 THE VOICE OF THE TRAVELER WHO ESCAPED

No matter how exhausted you are,
and though you think you will die of thirst,
do not enter the house in the forest.
Ignore the unlocked door
and the lamp in the window, lit for you.
Pass the house, which is real
and warm and apparently safe,
where the traveler is received
by someone, or at least
by a fire and a spread table.
It is only when you finish eating
and, drowsy and grateful, pull off your shoes,
that the ax falls or the giant returns
or the monster springs or the witch
locks the door from the outside
and throws away the key.

2 WARNING TO VIRGINS

Each year you become more wary,
less easily taken in,
but my disguises still fool you.
Today I will go as the bear
who lumbers to the door
of two young beauties, to be brushed
and petted, and to eat
out of their hands. Yesterday
I was the prince of frogs
hopping up golden stairs
to sheets that smelled of the sun.
Tomorrow I'll live, an unspecified beast,
in a marvelous castle, enjoying
the echo chamber, my godlike roar.
You know the girl, and how

she will discover the human.
But I'm not through; I'll come
and trick you, long-legged darling,
baby blond, with my wizened face,
my dwarf's cap and ridiculous voice.
Watch out for little men
at crossroads, who give you directions
and ask to share your supper:
one slip of the tongue, and you lose.
There is no second chance.

3   A VOICE FROM OUT OF THE NIGHT

Remember me, I was a celebrity,
the famous beauty. All mirrors confirmed me,
the panel of judges ogled me
and cast a unanimous vote.
I was asked my opinion
on marriage, men, abortion,
the use of liquor and drugs;
that was a long time ago.

When my voice deepened
and a bristle
appeared under my chin,
when my blond hair
developed gray roots
and my waist thickened,
the rumors started.
When my legs became sticks
and small brown toads
spotted the backs of my hands,
everyone believed them.
I was accused of devouring children
and mutilating men;
they said I smelled of old age
and strong home remedies.
They cast me into the forest
but come to me secretly, in the dark,
in their times of trouble.
What could I have done to convince them
I was not guilty?

Loss of beauty was all
the proof they needed.

Young wives in love with your men,
kissing your babies: this
could be a warning, but what is the use?
Husbands will flee you,
sons will turn on you,
daughters will throw up their hands
and cry, "Not me! Not me!"

4   THE HUNTER'S VOICE

Happily, I am exempt
from your bazaar of punishments
and rewards, the way you pass out beauty
and hold the burning shoes in abeyance
until the pendulum swings.
I will accept an assignment
from anyone who pays me,
and if the heart I bring back as proof
is not the intended one,
who is to know? I wear green,
not your colors of blood and snow;
I disappear among trees
and am not missed.
You would never believe
I have changed the plot of your lives.

5   THE FALSE BRIDE'S SIDE OF THE STORY

Kindness ran in your blood,
poverty spiked mine.

Nature gave you beauty,
mine came from tubes of paint.

You were a trusting fool,
I tried to take care of myself.

You wept genuine diamonds,
I wept plain salt tears.

You kept warm in a paper dress,
I froze in furs and woolens.

You found love without trying,
I took your lover but failed at love.

Your wedding ring kept shining,
mine turned black the first night.

Your baby was plump and bright-eyed,
mine was a monster disguised as a child.

Sister, my soul, my twin
on the other end of our seesaw,
any moment now
you will rise to the top, resurrected,
your cheeks swelling like plums,
while I go down to my death.
There the story breaks off
for the sake of the children who listen,
but don't be too sure. One day,
one afternoon, as you sit
(a calm Vermeer in sunlight)
counting your blessings like stitches,
I may step out of the sun,
large and dark as life.

6   THE THIRD SON'S CONFESSION

Early on I was chosen
the one least likely to succeed.
I was made fun of, but got away
with daydreaming and learning the language
of wood doves and white snakes.
My brothers were ambitious
and steady; they made maps
of possible trails through the forest,
they trained for months
for the climb up the glass mountain,
they monitored their shudders
to overcome fear on the field of bones.
I wished them luck, but they failed,
they came home defeated and bitter,
and I, late bloomer intending nothing,
found myself on the other side
of the forest, across the boneyard,
on top of the glass mountain.
Don't ask me if I was chosen
or simply lucky. Years ago

137

I threw a penny down a well,
but I've forgotten the wish.

7   FLESH AND BLOOD

This is my brother the fat, caged boy
This is my brother the spotted fawn
These are my brothers the seven ravens
These are my brothers the six mute swans

I have a plan for my brother the boy
I have a hermit's shack for my fawn
I've cut off a finger to save my ravens
I've given up speech to save my swans

"Help me," whispers my brother the boy
"Play with me," begs my high-stepping fawn
"Why were you born," lament the ravens
"You caused our exile," accuse the swans

Brothers, my brothers, I am your sister
I am a woman, I will be a wife
I am your face in the altered mirror
I will give you back your life

Brother my boy, you'll grow thin and forget me
You'll play with another, brother my fawn
Human, my seven, you will hunt ravens
Human, you'll leave me, my six mute swans

8   THE VOICE FROM UNDER THE HAZEL BUSH

I died for you. Each spring
I wake in my house of roots;
my memory leafs out
into a rich green dress
for you to dance in. The moon
turns it to silver, the evening sun
to gold. Be happy, my daughter.
You think I have magic powers,
others call it love.
I tell you it is the will
to survive, in you, in the earth.
Your story does not end
with the wedding dance, it goes on.

THE TRIUMPH OF LIFE: MARY SHELLEY

The voice addressing us is that of Mary Wollstonecraft Shelley (1797–1851), daughter of the radical philosopher William Godwin and the feminist Mary Wollstonecraft, who died as a result of her birth. She eloped with Percy Shelley, who was married to Harriet Westbrook at the time, and became his second wife after Harriet committed suicide. Shelley and Mary lived a nomadic life, moving around England and the Continent, never settling down anywhere for long. Three of their four children died in infancy. Their eight years together were a series of crises, many of them brought about by Shelley's restlessness and the drain of outsiders on their emotional and physical resources. After Shelley's accidental drowning, Mary, who was twenty-four at the time of his death, supported herself and their surviving son by her own writing and by editing and annotating Shelley's work. She published the first complete edition of his poems. Her own works consist of essays, short stories, and six novels, of which *Frankenstein,* written when she was nineteen, is the most famous. Her journal has been an important biographical source for Shelley's and her life together.

I

My father taught me to think,
to value mind over body,
to refuse even the airiest cage

to be a mouth as well as an ear,
to ask difficult questions,
not to marry because I was asked,
not to believe in heaven

None of this kept me from bearing
four children and losing three
by the time I was twenty-two

He wanted to think I sprang
from his head like the Greek goddess

He forgot that my mother died
of my birth, *The Rights of Women*
washed away in puerperal blood,
and that I was her daughter too

2

I met him when I was sixteen
He came to sit at my father's feet
and stayed to sit at mine

We became lovers
who remained friends
even after we married

A marriage of true minds
It is what you want
It is what we wanted

We did not believe in power
We were gentle
We shared our bodies with others
We thought we were truly free

My father taught us there was a solution
to everything, even evil

We were generous, honest
We thought we had the solution

and still, a woman walked
into the water because of us

3

After that death I stopped
believing in solutions

And when my children died
it was hard not to suspect
there was a god, a judgment

For months I wanted to be
with those three small bodies,
to be still in a dark place

No more mountain passes
No more flight from creditors

with arms as long as our bills
No more games to find out
who was the cleverest of us all
No more ghost stories by the fire
with my own ghosts at the window,
smiles sharpened like sickles
on the cold stone of the moon

For months I made a fortress
of my despair
"A defect of temper," they called it
His biographers never liked me

You would have called it a sickness,
given me capsules and doctors,
brushes and bright paints,
kits for paper flowers

4

An idea whose time has come,
you say about your freedom
but you forget the reason

Shall I remind you of history,
of choice and chance, the wish and the world,
of courage and locked doors,
biology and fate?

I wanted what you want,
what you have

If I could have chosen my children
and seen them survive
I might have believed in equality,
written your manifestos

Almost two hundred years
of medical science divide us

5

And yet, my father was right
It was the spirit that won in the end

After the sea had done
what it could to his flesh
I knew he was my husband
only by the books
in his pockets: Sophocles, Keats

The word survives the body

It was then I decided
not to marry again
but to live for the word

6

I allowed his body to be burned
on that Italian beach
Rome received his ashes

You have read that our friend
snatched his heart from the fire
You call it a grisly act,
something out of my novel

You don't speak of the heart
in your letters, your sharp-eyed poems
You speak about your bodies
as though they had no mystery,
no caves, no sudden turnings

You claim isolation, night sweats,
hanging on by your teeth

You don't trust the heart
though you define death
as the absence of heartbeat

You would have taken a ring,
a strand of hair, a shoelace—
a symbol, a souvenir

not the center, the real thing

7

He died
and the world gave no outward sign

I started a Journal of Sorrow

But there were the words, the poems,
passion and ink spilling
over the edges of all those sheets
There was the hungry survivor
of our bodily life together

Would it have lasted, our marriage,
if he had stayed alive?

As it was, we fed each other
like a pair of thrushes
I gave his words to the world
and they came back to me
as bread and meat and apples,
art and nature, mind and flesh
keeping each other alive

His last, unfinished poem
was called "The Triumph of Life"

8

You are surprised at my vision,
that a nineteen-year-old girl
could have written that novel,
how much I must have known

But I only wanted to write
a tale to tremble by,
what is oddly called a romance

By accident I slid
out of my century
into yours of white-coated men
in underground installations,
who invent their own destruction
under fluorescent lights

And in a few more decades,
when your test-tube babies sprout,
you will call me the prophet
of ultimate horror again

It was only a private nightmare
that dreamed the arrogance of your time

I was not your Cassandra
In any age, life has to be lived
before we can know what it is

The Story

You are telling a story:
How Fire Took Water to Wife

It's always like this, you say,
opposites attract

They want to enter each other,
be one,
so he burns her as hard as he can
and she tries to drown him

It's called love at first
and doesn't hurt

but after a while she weeps
and says he is killing her,
he shouts that he cannot breathe
underwater—

Make up your own
ending, you say to the children,
and they will, they will

THE ARTIST'S MODEL, *CA.* 1912

In 1886 I came apart—

I who had been Mme. Rivière,
whole under flowing silk,
had sat on the grass, naked,
my body an unbroken invitation—

splintered into thousands
of particles, a bright rock
blasted to smithereens;
even my orange skirt dissolved
into drops that were not orange.

Now they are stacking me like a child's
red and blue building blocks,
splitting me down the middle,
blackening half my face;

they tell me the world has changed,
haven't I heard, and give me
a third eye, a rooster's beak.

I ask for my singular name
back, but they say in the future
only my parts will be known,
a gigantic pair of lips,
a nipple, slick as candy,

and that even those will disappear,
white on white or black on black,
and you will look for me
in the air, in the absence of figure,
in space, inside your head,
where I started, your own work of art.

The End of Science Fiction

This is not fantasy, this is our life.
We are the characters
who have invaded the moon,
who cannot stop their computers.
We are the gods who can unmake
the world in seven days.

Both hands are stopped at noon.
We are beginning to live forever,
in lightweight, aluminum bodies
with numbers stamped on our backs.
We dial our words like Muzak.
We hear each other through water.

The genre is dead. Invent something new.
Invent a man and a woman
naked in a garden,
invent a child that will save the world,
a man who carries his father
out of a burning city.
Invent a spool of thread
that leads a hero to safety,
invent an island on which he abandons
the woman who saved his life
with no loss of sleep over his betrayal.

Invent us as we were
before our bodies glittered
and we stopped bleeding:
invent a shepherd who kills a giant,
a girl who grows into a tree,
a woman who refuses to turn
her back on the past and is changed to salt,
a boy who steals his brother's birthright
and becomes the head of a nation.

Invent real tears, hard love,
slow-spoken, ancient words,
difficult as a child's
first steps across a room.

What Will You Do

What did you do when the glacier
paved your mouth with ice
   when your scales fell off
and were left on the ground to rust
   when you stopped treading water
and started breathing air

What did you do when you realized
you were different from the others
   when you were cheated of your fur
your prehensile tail
   when death revealed itself
as the Supreme Being
unappeasable

And what did you do when the sun
stopped revolving around you
   when animals started to disappear
and the trees loosened their roots
imperceptibly at first
so you would not notice
   when water declared an eye for an eye
and pumped your poison back into you

and when your children left you
and joined the enemy
   when the air became colder and colder
and you moved faster than sound
though your love letter never got there
   what did you do when history
fell down at your feet
and asked to start all over

That's what you will do

WHY WE TELL STORIES

For Linda Nemec Foster

Because we used to have leaves
and on damp days
our muscles feel a tug,
painful now, from when roots
pulled us into the ground

and because our children believe
they can fly, an instinct retained
from when the bones in our arms
were shaped like zithers and broke
neatly under their feathers

and because before we had lungs
we knew how far it was to the bottom
as we floated open-eyed
like painted scarves through the scenery
of dreams, and because we awakened

and learned to speak

2

We sat by the fire in our caves,
and because we were poor, we made up a tale
about a treasure mountain
that would open only for us

and because we were always defeated,
we invented impossible riddles
only we could solve,
monsters only we could kill,
women who could love no one else

and because we had survived
sisters and brothers, daughters and sons,

we discovered bones that rose
from the dark earth and sang
as white birds in the trees

3

Because the story of our life
becomes our life

Because each of us tells
the same story
but tells it differently

and none of us tells it
the same way twice

Because grandmothers looking like spiders
want to enchant the children
and grandfathers need to convince us
what happened happened because of them

and though we listen only
haphazardly, with one ear,
we will begin our story
with the word *and*

From *Second Language* (1986)

NECESSITIES

1

A map of the world. Not the one in the atlas,
but the one in our heads, the one we keep coloring in.
With the blue thread of the river by which we grew up.
The green smear of the woods we first made love in.
The yellow city we thought was our future.
The red highways not traveled, the green ones
with their missed exits, the black side roads
which took us where we had not meant to go.
The high peaks, recorded by relatives,
though we prefer certain unmarked elevations,
the private alps no one knows we have climbed.
The careful boundaries we draw and erase.
And always, around the edges,
the opaque wash of blue, concealing
the drop-off they have stepped into before us,
singly, mapless, not looking back.

2

The illusion of progress. Imagine our lives without it:
tape measures rolled back, yardsticks chopped off.
Wheels turning but going nowhere.
Paintings flat, with no vanishing point.
The plots of all novels circular;
page numbers reversing themselves past the middle.
The mountaintop no longer a goal,
merely the point between ascent and descent.
All streets looping back on themselves;
life as a beckoning road an absurd idea.
Our children refusing to grow out of their childhoods;
the years refusing to drag themselves
toward the new century.
And hope, the puppy that bounds ahead,
no longer a household animal.

3

Answers to questions, an endless supply.
New ones that startle, old ones that reassure us.
All of them wrong perhaps, but for the moment
solutions, like kisses or surgery.
Rising inflections countered by level voices,
words beginning with *w* hushed
by declarative sentences. The small, bold sphere
of the period chasing after the hook,
the doubter that walks on water
and treads air and refuses to go away.

4

Evidence that we matter. The crash of the plane
which, at the last moment, we did not take.
The involuntary turn of the head,
which caused the bullet to miss us.
The obscene caller who wakes us at midnight
to the smell of gas. The moon's
full blessing when we fell in love,
its black mood when it was all over.
Confirm us, we say to the world,
with your weather, your gifts, your warnings,
your ringing telephones, your long, bleak silences.

5

Even now, *the old things first things,*
which taught us language. Things of day and of night.
Irrational lightning, fickle clouds, the incorruptible moon.
Fire as revolution, grass as the heir
to all revolutions. Snow
as the alphabet of the dead, subtle, undeciphered.
The river as what we wish it to be.
Trees in their humanness, animals in their otherness.
Summits. Chasms. Clearings.
And stars, which gave us the word *distance,*
so we could name our deepest sadness.

VOYAGER

For my father, 1897–1976

No one's body could be that light,
not even after it burns—
I know this is not you,
has nothing to do with you

I know you stand on a ship
looking through the eyeholes
nearsighted and patient as always,
still knowing everything

No matter what language they speak,
the boatmen in the black barges
that pass you, you will answer

No matter what bundle of time
they inhabit, you will direct them,
warn them once more and once more in vain

You who changed countries more often than shoes
can step ashore anywhere;
loneliness is the anchor
you've always carried with you

*

The desert is what I would have spared you,
the wilderness after my mother died,
your fixed star

Everything could be borne,
all knowledge, all separation
except that final one

Slowly you turned to stone

And I, your daughter/keeper—
what did I know about
the sentience of stone?

I watered you with indignities
and tears, but you never bloomed

Now both of you have entered
the history of your photographs;
together, young and smiling,
you stand on the steps of Notre Dame
"These are my parents, friends, and children,"
I say, but it is hopeless

I want the impossible photograph,
one that would show the world
your trick, how you and she
pulled joy from any borrowed hat
or sleeve, a survivor's art

This is the hardest knowledge:
that no one will remember you
when your daughters are gone

*

Five years before you died
I took your picture;
you were wearing a dark jacket
and your hair was white

Now I hold the negative
up to the light and the sun streams through
as though it were Notre Dame again,
the rose window

You are changed, you wear
the pale clothes of summer,
your skin and hair are black

How can you see, your glasses
are whitewashed and there are holes
where your teeth used to be

Nevertheless you smile at me
across an enormous distance
as you have so many times
to let me know you have arrived

BREAD AND APPLES

In the tale
the apple tree rises before her,
not in an orchard,
but solitary and sudden
in a world she does not know
is supernatural. It asks
in an old woman's voice
to be relieved of its red-faced burden.
Further on, in a field,
she hears the terrified cries
of bread almost burned in its fireplace.
She does not ask who made bread
in an uninhabited wilderness.

So memory raises landmarks,
unbidden, out of place
and time. My father sits
in the long-discarded chair;
the pages of the history book
he leafs through keep springing back
to the beginning. He does not explain
his presence here. Without a question
I pull the bread from the ashes
and place it on the ground to cool.

THE GARDEN

I bring my mother back to life,
her eyes still green, still laughing,
She is still not fashionably thin.

She looks past me
for the girl
she left her old age to.
She does not recognize her
in me, a graying woman
older than she will ever be.

How strange that in the garden
of memory where she lives
nothing ever changes;
the heavy fruit
cannot pull the branches
any closer to the ground.

BLOOD ORANGES

In 1936, a child
in Hitler's Germany,
what did I know about the war in Spain?
Andalusia was a tango
on a windup gramophone,
Franco a hero's face in the paper.
No one told me about a poet
for whose sake I might have learned Spanish
bleeding to death on a barren hill.
All I knew of Spain
were those precious imported treats
we splurged on for Christmas.
I remember pulling the sections apart,
lining them up, sucking each one
slowly, so the red sweetness
would last and last—
while I was reading a poem
by a long-dead German poet
in which the woods stood safe
under the moon's milky eye
and the white fog in the meadows
aspired to become lighter than air.

Your Tired, Your Poor

1 ASYLUM

"I cannot ask you to paint the tops
of your bare mountains green
or gentle your coasts to lessen
my homesickness. Beggar, not chooser,
I hand you the life you say I must leave
at the border, bundled and tied.
You riffle through it without looking,
stamp it and put it out the back
for the trash collector. 'Next,' you call.

"I am free. I stand in the desert,
heavy with what I smuggled in
behind my eyes and under my tongue:
memory and language, my rod and staff,
my leper's rattle, my yellow star."

2 ENGLISH AS A SECOND LANGUAGE

The underpaid young teacher
prints the letters *t, r, e, e*
on the blackboard and imagines
forests and gardens springing up
in the tired heads of her students.

But they see only four letters:
a vertical beam weighed down
by a crushing crossbar
followed by a hook,
and after the hook, two squiggles,
arcane identical twins
which could be spying eyes
or ready fists, could be handles,
could be curled seedlings, could take root,
could develop leaves.

There comes a day when the trees
refuse to let you pass
until you name them. Stones
speak up and reveal themselves
as the poor of your new country.
Then you see that the moon
has chosen to follow you here
and find yourself humming the music
you stuffed your ears against.
You dream in rhyme, in a language
you never wanted to understand.
When you pick up the telephone,
the voices from home arrive
sighing, bent by the ocean.
Their letters bear postage stamps
that surprise you with their strange, bright birds.

IDENTICAL TWINS

When they walk past me in the park
I shiver, as if two black cats
had crossed my path. Uncanny,
as if I were seeing things.
As if I were seeing two of me,
myself and the one in the mirror,
who must also be the one
I talk to when I'm alone.
The one I call "you," who loves me
better than any lover.
It is as though these sisters,
who tie their shoes in the same double bows
and bite their fingernails
down to the same horizon
existed to expose
twinlessness as a sham,
to let us know they know
about our secret:
the lost, illicit other
kept under lock and key
in the last room of the mind.

These days, riding the subway
to work and back, I notice
that the passengers move their lips
ever so slightly. I watch them
lean into themselves
as if toward a voice,
and then turn to the window
to search the backlit face
in the black, speeding mirror.

SOUTHPAW

"Were you an only child?" she asks.
No, but you've always favored the dreamer,
the star pitcher who writes novels,
the prophet with the red armband,
the low notes of the piano,
the swimmer against the stream.

You learned the truth early, that handles
are on the other side,
that doors are hinged to slow your entrance
and gloves and gadgets are made for others,
but you know that the ancient tools—
jugs, spoons, hammers, rakes—
care only about your opposable thumb.

It's your birthright, the extra effort
you've secretly come to love.
"Left, left," the drill sergeant stutters,
and you smile like one of the chosen.
You push the reluctant ballpoint
forward, while the letters wave back,
and taste the word *sinister* on your tongue.
How enchanting it is, so sensuous,
the song of a mermaid with two left arms.

After Whistler

There are girls who should have been swans.
At birth their feathers are burned;
their human skins never fit.
When the other children
line up on the side of the sun,
they will choose the moon,
that precious aberration.
They are the daughters mothers
worry about. All summer,
dressed in gauze, they flicker
inside the shaded house,
drawn to the mirror, where their eyes,
two languid moths, hang dreaming.
It's winter they wait for, the first snowfall
with the steady interior hum
only they can hear;
they stretch their arms, as if they were wounded,
toward the bandages of snow.
Briefly, the world is theirs
in its perfect frailty.

The Questioning

Mute and dazed, she has surfaced
in Memphis, Tennessee.
A squad car brought her in
just before dawn, before the sun
could turn its searchlight on her
and make her run. Fourteen,
perhaps fifteen, they think.
When they ask her about the cigarette burns
on her arms and ankles, she shakes her head.
She will not betray her keeper,
nor the location of hell.
When they offer her food, she suspects a trick.
For months or years she waited
for the rescue that did not come,
heard their feet overhead
coming and always going.
By now she denies them even her name.

No mother comes to claim her
and her emergence among us
does not explain the seasons.
It happens in autumn as well as spring;
it is happening now, somewhere
somebody's daughter comes stumbling
into the light, refusing
to give up her dark burden,
which is all she has brought from home.

WIDOW

What the neighbors bring to her kitchen
is food for the living. She wants to eat
the food of the dead, their pure
narcotic of dry, black seeds.
Why, without him, should she desire
the endurance offered by meat and grain,
the sugars that glue the soul to the body?
She thanks them, but does not eat,
consumes strong coffee as if it were air
and she the vigilant candle
on a famous grave, until the familiar
sounds of the house become strange,
turn into messages in the new language
he has been forced to learn.
All night she works on the code,
almost happy, her body rising
like bread, while the food in its china caskets
dries out on the kitchen table.

The Exhibit

My uncle in East Germany
points to the unicorn in the painting
and explains it is now extinct.
We correct him, say such a creature
never existed. He does not argue,
but we know he does not believe us.
He is certain power and gentleness
must have gone hand in hand
once. A prisoner of war
even after the war was over,
my uncle needs to believe in something
that could not be captured except by love,
whose single luminous horn
redeemed the murderous forest
and, dipped into foul water,
would turn it pure. This world,
this terrible world we live in,
is not the only possible one,
his eighty-year-old eyes insist,
dry wells that fill so easily now.

LETTER TO CALIFORNIA

We write to each other as if
we were using the same language,
though we are not. Your sentences lap
over each other like the waves
of the Pacific, strictureless;
your long, sleek-voweled words
fill my mouth like ripe avocados.
To read you is to dismiss
news of earthquakes and mud slides,
to imagine time in slow motion.
It is to think of the sun
as a creature that will not let anything
happen to you.
                    Back here
we grow leeks and beans and sturdy
roots that will keep for months.
We have few disasters; *i.e.,*
no grandeur to speak of. Instead
we engage in a low-keyed continuous struggle
to get through the winter, which swallows
two seasons and throws its shadow
over a third. How do you manage
without snow to tell you that you are mortal?
We are brought up short by a wind
that shapes our words; they fall
in clean, blunt strokes. The birds here
are mostly chickadees
and juncos, monochromes
bred to the long view
like the sky under siege of lead
and the bony trees, which hold
the dancer's first position
month after month. But we have
our intimations: now and then
a cardinal with its lyric call,
its body blazing like a saint's

unexpectedly gaudy heart,
spills on our reasonable scene
of brown and gray, unconscious of itself.
I search the language for a word
to tell you how red is red.

METAPHOR

For Gregory Orr, who asked, "How can one teach
'Spring and Fall: To a Young Child' in the Hawaiian Islands?"

Your question persists, like the scent
of ginger blossoms, like the remembered
banyan trees whose aerated roots
seize the earth like the claws of a cast-out god.
How, in a place where *winter* means
a token lessening, an almost unnoticed
handicap on profusion,
like quiet stages inside our bodies,
which mean adjustment but not death,
not even simulation of death.
Not like snow, the old metaphor
for the bleached shroud; not like the trees
outside my window, all bare bones,
those terrible reminders
which also comfort in their mute
indifference. Yesterday
it was 80° in Honolulu,
while here in the frozen grass
a hungry owl dug its claws
into a rabbit in broad daylight.
But that's taxonomy; change the names
and you have a tropical bird and its prey.
No difference there. And perhaps
the shock and clatter of loosening leaves
is greater in the imagination
of those who live in paradise
than it is for us who see it happen,
just as we dream the plumage
of equinoctial parrots
even gaudier than it is,
and a deaf-blind child
imagined a Venice so splendid
she could not sleep all night.

Perhaps today a girl
who might have been your student

is driving around the island
changed. Someone she loved has died.
She stares at the prodigal trees,
the bold, insistent flowers,
but all she sees is a bitter landscape:
goldengrove unleaving.
bare ruin'd choirs, where late the sweet birds sang.

STORM

To see the lightning
as a question mark
made by a trembling hand

and hear the thunder
as its dreaded answer,
ambiguous in the distance
but, close, a rebuke as brutal
as a clean blow to the head—

such childish superstition
comes back to you at night
when you lie still, enduring
the bludgeoning of the fissured dark,
still powerless, still guilty.

ACCOMMODATIONS

The house painter is not sentimental
and sets the wasp's nest on fire,
and the tribe of wasps is not proud
or dissuadable, and soon
a new nest hangs overhead.
We walk in and out of the door
under their home, a sponge
with oversized holes, quite safe,
keeping our downstairs distance
from their upstairs goings-on.

We're busy chasing a squirrel
which terrorizes our undersized
black-and-white cat, whose heart
pummels all parts of her body,
demanding an out, until she falls
on the red terrace. I want to poison
the squirrel, but of course I don't,
and the cat recovers and looks with desire
at the aspens, which have grown so tall—

up from the scarred, old bark
near the ground, to the milky skin
with its irregular love bites
above, where the birds keep climbing
nearer and nearer the sun,
our ancient, hovering nurse,
scatterbrained but intact
and close enough for comfort.

FOR THE STRANGERS

Even this late in the century
it's hard to think of them
as simply creatures with feathered caps
and matchstick bones arranged into wings,
a species that never carried
our secrets in their gravelly craws
or under their downy shoulders
and, though their eyes are glazed,
never flew high enough
to share the altitude of the dead.

Of course we've known for a long time
that no painted god of the sun
or lover gone south received our message,
the one we never could find
the exact words for,
that it was a mistake
to confuse our perpetual hunger
for distance with their nature.

Keats knew it too, when he took his grief
to the deaf but convenient nightingale.
The fiction of metaphor saved us
from madness, perhaps from crime,
certainly from the despair
of admitting the broken connection,
that the world resists meaning
not to tease us, but because
there is no meaning
except the one we invent.

And where does that leave us now—
where does it leave me each October
when hundreds of blackbirds interrupt
their journey for a rest
in my backyard, when they could have chosen

to unsettle the neighbors
with their massive, earsplitting presence?
I was born too late to believe in election.

When they return to the sky,
composing themselves in the ancient pen strokes
that will carry them forward
into the twenty-first century,
I stand and stare at their far-flung
unreadable signature.
No intention, I tell myself,
this is no sign; but the habit
of homage persists, the upturned face,
the eyes glossed with astonishment.

Up North

Already they are flying back,
gray clumps with nervous wings,
always the first to know.

Otherwise, mere inklings.
An occasional fiery branch
flags us down from the green,
but the leaves still rub soft-skinned
against each other, and the tomatoes
dawdle as though red
were a suitor willing to wait.
The trunks of the birches are lit
from within, like ideal nudes
who have no season. We lie
body to body under the trees
as we did last summer. Nothing has changed.
I search your face for the year,
but my eyes have aged at the same rate
and I've learned nothing. Plums
on the table beside us hoard
their juice inside sealed barrels
of gleaming skin, but you and I
don't hoard our sweetness, hoard anything.

SCENIC ROUTE

For Lucy, who called them "ghost houses"

Someone was always leaving
and never coming back.
The wooden houses wait like old wives
along this road; they are everywhere,
abandoned, leaning, turning gray.

Someone always traded
the lonely beauty
of hemlock and stony lakeshore
for survival, packed up his life
and drove off to the city.
In the yards the apple trees
keep hanging on, but the fruit
grows smaller year by year.

When we come this way again
the trees will have gone wild,
the houses collapsed, not even worth
the human act of breaking in.
Fields will have taken over.

What we will recognize
is the wind, the same fierce wind,
which has no history.

REASONS FOR NUMBERS

1

Because I exist

2

Because there must be a reason
why I should cast a shadow

3

So that good can try to be better
and become best
and beginning grow into middle and end

4

So the round earth can have its corners
and the house will not fall down around me

So the seasons will go on holding hands
and the string quartet play forever

5

For the invention of Milton and Shakespeare
and the older invention
of the wild rose, mother
to the petals
of my hand

6

Because
five
senses
are

not
enough

7

Because luck
is always odd

and the division
of history
into lean and fat
                    years
mysterious

8

To make the spider
possible
and the black ball which tells me
the game is up

but also to let
the noise of the world
make itself heard
as music

9

For the orbit of Jupiter
                Saturn
                Venus
                Mars
                Mercury
                Uranus
                Mickey Mantle
                Lou Gehrig
                Babe Ruth

10

Created functionless, for the sheer play
of the mind in its tens of thousands of moves

There is nothing like it in nature

THE POSSESSIVE CASE

Your father's mustache
My brother's keeper
La plume de ma tante
Le monocle de mon oncle
His Master's Voice
Son of a bitch
Charley's Aunt
Lady Chatterley's Lover
    The Prince of Wales
    The Duchess of Windsor
    The Count of Monte Cristo
    The Emperor of Ice Cream
    The Marquis de Sade
    The Queen of the Night
        Mozart's Requiem
        Beethoven's Ninth
        Bach's B-Minor Mass
        Schubert's Unfinished
        Krapp's Last Tape
        Custer's Last Stand
        Howards End
        Finnegans Wake
            The March of Time
            The Ides of March
            The Auroras of Autumn
            The winter of our discontent
            The hounds of spring
            The Hound of Heaven
        Dante's Inferno
        Vergil's Aeneid
        Homer's Iliad
    The Fall of the City
    The Decline of the West
    The Birth of a Nation
The Declaration of Independence
The ride of Paul Revere
The Pledge of Allegiance

The Spirit of '76
    The Age of Reason
    The Century of the Common Man
    The Psychopathology of Everyday Life
        Portnoy's Complaint
        Whistler's Mother
        The Sweetheart of Sigma Chi
        The whore of Babylon
        The Bride of Frankenstein
        The French Lieutenant's Woman
            A Room of One's Own
            Bluebeard's Castle
            Plato's cave
            Santa's workshop
            Noah's ark
            The House of the Seven Gables
        The Dance of the Seven Veils
        Anitra's Dance
        The Moor's Pavane
        My Papa's Waltz
    Your father's mustache

STALKING THE POEM

1

Only one word will do. It isn't on the tip of your tongue, but you know it's not far. It's the one fish that won't swim into your net, a figure that hides in a crowd of similar figures, a domino stone in the face-down pool. Your need to find it becomes an obsession, single-minded and relentless as lust. It's a long time before you can free yourself, let it go. "Forget it," you say, and think that you do. When the word is sure you have forgotten it, it comes out of hiding. But it isn't taking any chances even now and has prepared its appearance with care. It surrounds itself with new and inconspicuous friends and faces you in a showup line in which everyone looks equally innocent. Of course you know it instantly, the way Joan of Arc knew the Dauphin and Augustine knew God. You haven't been so happy in weeks. You rush the word to your poem, which had died for lack of it, and it arises pink-cheeked as Lazarus. The two of you share the wine.

2

You've got the poem cornered. It gives up, lies down, plays dead. No more resistance. How easily you could take it into your teeth and walk off with it! But you are afraid of the sound they will make crunching the bones. You are afraid of the taste of blood, of the poem's dark, unknown insides. So you stand above it, sniffing its fur, poking and pushing it, turning it over. Suddenly you see that its eyes are open and that they stare at you with contempt. You walk away with your tail between your legs. When you return the poem has disappeared.

3

The poem is complete in your head, its long, lovely shape black against the white space in your mind. Each line is there, secure, re-callable, pulled forth by the line before it and the one before that, like a melody whose second part you can sing once you have sung the first, but not before. All there, all perfectly linked. But when you pick up the pen, the shape dissolves, pales, spreads into slovenliness. You feel the poem escaping; you can't write fast enough. By some miracle you recover all the bits and pieces, and you man- age to put them in their proper order. You have been saved, you think. But the poem is not the beautiful figure you held in your mind. It is gawky and gap-toothed, its arms are too long for its body, its clothes don't fit. It looks up at you from the page accusingly. Look at the mess you've made, it says. See what you can do with me: last chance, don't blow it. Filled with gratitude, you roll up your sleeves and go to work.

Monet Refuses the Operation

Doctor, you say there are no halos
around the streetlights in Paris
and what I see is an aberration
caused by old age, an affliction.
I tell you it has taken me all my life
to arrive at the vision of gas lamps as angels,
to soften and blur and finally banish
the edges you regret I don't see,
to learn that the line I called the horizon
does not exist and sky and water,
so long apart, are the same state of being.
Fifty-four years before I could see
Rouen cathedral is built
of parallel shafts of sun,
and now you want to restore
my youthful errors: fixed
notions of top and bottom,
the illusion of three-dimensional space,
wisteria separate
from the bridge it covers.
What can I say to convince you
the Houses of Parliament dissolve
night after night to become
the fluid dream of the Thames?
I will not return to a universe
of objects that don't know each other,
as if islands were not the lost children
of one great continent. The world
is flux, and light becomes what it touches,
becomes water, lilies on water,
above and below water,
becomes lilac and mauve and yellow
and white and cerulean lamps,
small fists passing sunlight
so quickly to one another
that it would take long, streaming hair

inside my brush to catch it.
To paint the speed of light!
Our weighted shapes, these verticals,
burn to mix with air
and change our bones, skin, clothes
to gases. Doctor,
if only you could see
how heaven pulls earth into its arms
and how infinitely the heart expands
to claim this world, blue vapor without end.

What Is Left to Say

The self steps out of the circle;
it stops wanting to be
the farmer, the wife, and the child.

It stops trying to please
by learning everyone's dialect;
it finds it can live, after all,
in a world of strangers.

It sends itself fewer flowers;
it stops preserving its tears in amber.

How splendidly arrogant it was
when it believed the gold-filled tomb
of language awaited its raids!
Now it frequents the junkyards,
knowing all words are secondhand.

It has not chosen its poverty,
this new frugality.
It did not want to fall out of love
with itself. Young,
it celebrated itself
and richly sang itself,
seeing only itself
in the mirror of the world.

It cannot return. It assumes
its place in a universe of stars
that do not see it. Even the dead
no longer need it to be at peace.
Its function is to applaud.

THERE ARE MORNINGS

Even now, when the plot
calls for me to turn to stone,
the sun intervenes. Some mornings
in summer I step outside
and the sky opens
and pours itself into me
as if I were a saint
about to die. But the plot
calls for me to live,
be ordinary, say nothing
to anyone. Inside the house
the mirrors burn when I pass.

FUGITIVE

My life is running away with me;
the two of us are in cahoots.
I hold still while it paints
dark circles under my eyes,
streaks my hair gray, stuffs pillows
under my dress. In each new room
the mirror reassures me
I'll not be recognized.
I'm learning to travel light,
like the juice in the power line.
My baggage, swallowed by memory,
weighs almost nothing. No one suspects
its value. When they knock on my door,
badges flashing, I open up:
I don't match their description.
"Wrong room," they say, and apologize.
My life in the corner winks
and wipes off my fingerprints.

A Day like Any Other

Such insignificance: a glance
at your record on the doctor's desk
or a letter not meant for you.
How could you have known? It's not true
that your life passes before you
in rapid motion, but your watch
suddenly ticks like an amplified heart,
the hands freezing against a white
that is a judgment. Otherwise, nothing.
The face in the mirror is still yours.
Two men pass on the sidewalk
and do not stare at your window.
Your room is silent, the plants
locked inside their mysterious lives
as always. The queen of the night
refuses to bloom, does not accept
your definition. It makes no sense,
your scanning the street for a traffic snarl,
a new crack in the pavement,
a flag at half-mast—signs
of some disturbance in the world,
some recognition that the sun
has turned its dark face toward you.

INTO SPACE

How light we are becoming

Our diets of greens and seeds
hollow us, bring us closer
to the birds;
our buoyant winter coats
are stuffed for luck
with incipient feathers.

Everything in our lives
is thinning down, prepares itself
for the weightless future.

Lasers replace cumbersome tools,
boxes diminish to buttons;
soon our messy, erroneous hearts
will be superseded
and the gigantic god
of history dwarfed to a nylon tape
we carry in our pockets.

*

Like mountain climbers and athletes,
we undergo daily training

We go out in the morning
and when we return
our houses are thirty stories high,
our names not listed
in the lobby

We float to the top of the building,
naked in glass elevators,
and when we emerge our neighbors
meet us with guns, just in case

They look at us round-eyed
and ask who we are

Back on the street, our feet
lift off the ground, the trees
and lampposts we reach for back off
into the painted distance

*

In a recurrent dream
I am asked to step out of my shoes,
fold and stack my clothes,
place the contents of my purse
on a desk for later disposal.
I leave my daughter's photographed hands,
my other daughter's new poem,
my keys, my driver's license
with the bad picture, my Chinese
address book with its birds and flowers.
Strip-searched, I am forced to surrender
my mother's bookmark of dried heather
taped to the sole of my foot
and my husband's twenty-year-old face
in a heart-shaped locket concealed in my hair.
Finally, when I step on the scales
no lights flash;
the X-ray scanner sweeps over me
and finds me empty.

*

Think of the sac of memory
as the last resort,
the bundle the refugees tie to a stick
when they cross the frozen river

Think of the contents, volatile
as dandelion fluff
when we finally scatter it
into the atmosphere we are leaving

Think of it falling on someone
who suspects nothing,
who is suddenly moved to recall
a forgotten childhood scene
and finds himself stunned by its gravity.

FROM *WAVING FROM SHORE* (1989)

MISSING THE DEAD

I miss the old scrawl on the viaduct,
the crazily dancing red letters: BIRD LIVES.
It's gone now, the wall as clean as forgetting.
I go home and put on a record,
Charlie Parker Live at the Blue Note.
Each time I play it, months or years apart,
the music emerges more luminous;
I never listened so well before.

I wish my parents had been musicians
and left me themselves transformed into sound,
or that I could believe in the stars
as the radiant bodies of the dead.
Then I could stand in the dark, pointing out
my mother and father to all
who did not know them, how they shimmer,
how they keep getting brighter
as we keep moving toward each other.

WHEN I AM ASKED

When I am asked
how I began writing poems,
I talk about the indifference of nature.

It was soon after my mother died,
a brilliant June day,
everything blooming.

I sat on a gray stone bench
in a lovingly planted garden,
but the day lilies were as deaf
as the ears of drunken sleepers
and the roses curved inward.
Nothing was black or broken
and not a leaf fell
and the sun blared endless commercials
for summer holidays.

I sat on a gray stone bench
ringed with the ingenue faces
of pink and white impatiens
and placed my grief
in the mouth of language,
the only thing that would grieve with me.

JOY

"Don't cry, it's only music,"
someone's voice is saying.
"No one you love is dying."

It's only music. And it was only spring,
the world's unreasoning body
run amok, like a saint's, with glory,
that overwhelmed a young girl
into unreasoning sadness.
"Crazy," she told herself,
"I should be dancing with happiness."

But it happened again. It happens
when we make bottomless love—
there follows a bottomless sadness
which is not despair
but its nameless opposite.
It has nothing to do with the passing of time.
It's not about loss. It's about
two seemingly parallel lines
suddenly coming together
inside us, in some place
that is still wilderness.

Joy, joy, the sopranos sing,
reaching for the shimmering notes
while our eyes fill with tears.

CAVALLERIA RUSTICANA

All the fireflies in the world
are gathered in our yard tonight,
flickering in the shrubs
like an ostentatious display
of Christmas lights out of season.
But the music in the air
is the music of heat, of August—
cicadas scraping out
their thin, harsh treble
like country fiddlers settling in
for a long night. I feel at home
with their relentless tune,
minimalist, like the eighties.

Events repeat themselves,
but with a difference that makes all
the difference. As a child,
one summer night in Verona
at my first opera,
I watched a swarm of matches
light up the Roman arena
until we were silent. It was as if
music were a night-blooming flower
that would not open
until we held our breath.
Then the full-blown sound,
the single-minded combat
of passion: voices sharpening
their glittering blades on one another,
electing to live or die.
It was that simple. The story was
of no importance, the motive lost
in the sufficient, breathing dark.
If there was a moon I don't remember.

MAGNOLIA

This year spring and summer decided
to make it quick, roll themselves into one
season of three days
and steam right out of winter.
In the front yard the reluctant
magnolia buds lost control
and suddenly stood wide open.
Two days later their pale pink silks
heaped up around the trunk
like cast-off petticoats.

Remember how long spring used to take?
And how long from the first locking of fingers
to the first real kiss? And after that
the other eternity, endless motion
toward the undoing of a button?

VISITING MY NATIVE COUNTRY WITH MY AMERICAN-BORN HUSBAND

I am as much of a stranger
in this particular town
as he is. But when we walk
along the Neckar, an old folk song
comes back to me and I sing it to him
without a slip. In the restaurant
I notice my voice and my gestures
are like those of the women around me.
He watches me change contours
in the polished concave of his spoon;
he stirs his coffee and I dissolve.
When I come back I look different,
while he remains what he is,
what he always was.

LATE HOURS

On summer nights the world
moves within earshot
on the interstate with its swish
and growl, an occasional siren
that sends chills through us.
Sometimes, on clear, still nights,
voices float into our bedroom,
lunar and fragmented,
as if the sky had let them go
long before our birth.

In winter we close the windows
and read Chekhov,
nearly weeping for his world.

What luxury, to be so happy
that we can grieve
over imaginary lives.

POEM FOR MY BIRTHDAY

I have stopped being the heroine
of my bad dreams. The melodramas
of betrayal and narrow escapes
from which I wake up grateful
for an unexciting life
are starring my troubled young friend
or one of my daughters. I'm not the one
who swims too far out to sea;
I am the one who waves from shore
vainly and in despair.
Life is what happens to someone else;
I stand on the sidelines and wring my hands.
Strange that my dreams should have accepted
the minor role I've been cast in
by stories since stories began.
Does that mean I have solved my life?
I'm still afraid in my dreams, but not for myself.
Fear gets rededicated
with a new stone that bears a needier name.

BEDTIME STORY

The moon lies on the river
like a drop of oil.
The children come to the banks to be healed
of their wounds and bruises.
The fathers who gave them their wounds and bruises
come to be healed of their rage.
The mothers grow lovely; their faces soften,
the birds in their throats awake.
They all stand hand in hand
and the trees around them,
forever on the verge
of becoming one of them,
stop shuddering and speak their first word.

But that is not the beginning.
It is the end of the story,
and before we come to the end,
the mothers and fathers and children
must find their way to the river,
separately, with no one to guide them.
That is the long, pitiless part,
and it will scare you.

VIRTUOSI

In memory of my parents

People whose lives have been shaped
by history—and it is always tragic—
do not want to talk about it,
would rather dance, give parties
on thrift-shop china. You feel
wonderful in their homes,
two leaky rooms, nests
they stowed inside their hearts
on the road into exile.
They know how to fix potato peelings
and apple cores so you smack your lips.

The words *start over again*
hold no terror for them.
Obediently they rise
and go with only a rucksack
or tote bag. If they weep,
it's when you're not looking.

To tame their nightmares, they choose
the most dazzling occupations,
swallow the flames in the sunset sky,
jump through burning hoops
in their elegant tiger suits.
Cover your eyes: there's one
walking on a thread
thirty feet above us—
shivering points of light
leap across her body,
and she works without a net.

THREE POEMS
ABOUT THE VOICELESS

1

The voiceless wear scarves pulled tight
across their mouths, like the woman
on the commuter train
with the huge eyes and olive skin.
No English. Somehow she conveyed
that she had paid before getting on,
but she had no ticket. The conductor said
he wanted her name and address
so the railroad could send her a bill.
Her eyes went wild; the conductor
was wearing a uniform.
She shook her head: no English!
Her eyes above the muffler
darted from corner to corner
with the frantic speed of any small thing
that's trapped and cannot find an exit.

2

Sometimes the voiceless decide
to shield their eyes. At McDonald's
a man's hard gaze slides sideways
to check me out, and when I turn
the eyes go blank, freeze forward,
agates that have seen nothing.

On the bus it happens again,
different hair and clothes, same eyes;
secretive antennae
darting and gone, bars drawn
across the windows of the soul.

I stare at two missing children

on the poster above his head.
Their eyes are straight on me,
as if I were the camera
and trust still possible.

3

I've seen one of the voiceless
borrow the voice of the saxophone.
He stands on a downtown street
on a wintry, dull afternoon
blowing his heart out. His heart
slides down the tube of his instrument
and comes out in a long, sweet note,
excruciating and breathless,
like the harrowing pleasure of sex.
A voice made human, a language
all of us, shoppers, browsers,
and purse snatchers, understand.

Epilepsy, Petit Mal

There are times, each day, when their child leaves them—
briefly, for half a minute perhaps—
though she remains standing among them
with the toy or book she is holding.
Her body goes stiff, her pupils lock in position.
She cannot see them. All they can do is wait
until she is given back to them.
Then they ask her where she has been
and she answers, surprised, that she has been with them
the whole time. But they don't believe her;
they think she guards some fantastic secret,
a momentary vision of heaven
so intense that it stuns her. They cannot believe
the alternative, which is nothing—
those mock deaths, over and over, for nothing.

PAUL DELVAUX: *THE VILLAGE OF THE MERMAIDS*

Oil on canvas, 1943

Who is that man in black, walking
away from us into the distance?
The painter, they say, took a long time
finding his vision of the world.

The mermaids, if that is what they are
under their full-length skirts,
sit facing each other
all down the street, more of an alley,
in front of their gray row houses.
They all look the same, like a fair-haired
order of nuns, or like prostitutes
with chaste, identical faces.
How calm they are, with their vacant eyes,
their hands in laps that betray nothing.
Only one has scales on her dusky dress.

It is 1943; it is Europe,
and nothing fits. The one familiar figure
is the man in black approaching the sea,
and he is small and walking away from us.

APHASIA

It's not only because the world
is coming apart that it no longer
offers itself to me
as an infinite dictionary
and speech takes back its most glamorous figures.
Something in me, an alteration
like liquid turning solid,
draws me to the photograph
of the country woman whose mouth
has become a straight, hard line,
a terse signal for closure.
I try to imagine her younger,
her mouth swelling and parting
into lips, her nearly opaque eyes
fluid with expectation.
Clearly the world has never
offered itself to her;
it has taken and taken until she became
empty and sealed. The habit of speech
is not like riding a bicycle,
something you never forget;
it dries up like the habit of tears,
like playfulness. Nothing in her face
gives me permission to speak for her,
even if I could.

MARY

Mary points to a fellow patient
in the nursing home and says,
"She's always crying." The woman
is weeping bitterly.
I'm shocked because there's no hint
of compassion in Mary's face.
The callousness of the old, I think.
But then I realize that's not it.
Mary, deaf and in a wheelchair,
claims no more sympathy for herself,
accepts the world's indifference
as the natural order of things,
though her eyes still recognize kindness.
Death won't let anyone off the hook,
whether we rage or go gentle.
Mary's way is to let go,
little by little, of anger and love,
the self's constituents. She moves
toward death the way a swimmer
eases into freezing water:
ankles, knees, hips,
shivering rib cage, collarbone.

AFTER YOUR DEATH

The first time we said your name
you broke through the flat crust of your grave
and rose, a movable statue,
walking and talking among us.

Since then you've grown a little.
We keep you slightly larger
than life-size, reciting bits of your story,
our favorite odds and ends.
Of all your faces we've chosen one
for you to wear, a face wiped clean
of sadness. Now you have no other.

You're in our power. Do we
terrify you, do you wish
for another face? Perhaps
you want to be left in darkness.

But you have no say in the matter.
As long as we live, we keep you
from dying your real death,
which is being forgotten. We say,
we don't want to abandon you,
when we mean we can't let you go.

All Night

All night the knot in the shoelace
waits for its liberation,
and the match on the table packs its head
with anticipation of light.
The faucet sweats out a bead of water,
which gathers strength for the free fall,
while the lettuce in the refrigerator
succumbs to its brown killer.
And in the novel I put down
before I fall asleep,
the paneled walls of a room
are condemned to stand and wait
for tomorrow, when I'll get to the page
where the prisoner finds the secret door
and steps into air and the scent of lilacs.

THE DEAF DANCING TO ROCK

The eardrums of the deaf are already broken; they like it loud. They dance away the pain of silence, of a world where people laugh and wince and smirk and burst into tears over words they don't understand. As they dance the world reaches out to them, from the floor, from the vibrating walls. Now they hear the ongoing drone of a star in its nearly endless fall through space; they hear seedlings break through the crust of the earth in split-second thumps, and in another part of the world, the thud of billions of leaves hitting the ground, apart and together, in the intricate rhythmic patterns we cannot hear. Their feet, knees, hips, enact the rhythms of the universe. Their waving arms signal the sea and pull its great waves ashore.

FILM SCRIPT

A tall, redheaded woman
in a green shirt and white slacks
is walking along a deserted beach.
Her life has become a cruel riddle;
she thinks she may find the answer
in the sky or the sand. As she walks,
a bottle washes up before her
bare feet. She stoops and opens it,
pulls out the message. Staggers.
Stuffs it back in the bottle
and throws it out to sea,
a long, fierce, overhand throw.
Her face is pure terror. She turns around
and walks in the direction she came from,
as if there was still a chance to catch up
with her old life. She does not feel
the broken shells and slippery seaweed.
The sky maintains its bluish face
with the few bland summer clouds;
the sea remains placid. She feels herself
becoming lighter, losing ground;
her sandals drop from her hand,
her feet stop touching the sand. She is rising,
slowly at first. Her contours blur,
dissolve at the edges until she becomes
a low-lying cloud, a delicate shred of fog
that finally fills with consuming light,
and she is lost, like breath given back to the air.

TRIAGE

Bertolt Brecht lamented that he lived in an age when it was almost a crime to talk about trees, because that meant being silent about so much evil. Walking past a stand of tall, still healthy elms along Chicago's lakefront, I think of what Brecht said. I want to celebrate these elms which have been spared by the plague, these survivors of a once flourishing tribe commemorated by all the Elm Streets in America. But to celebrate them is to be silent about the people who sit and sleep underneath them, the homeless poor who are hauled away by the city like trash, except it has no place to dump them. To speak of one thing is to suppress another. When I talk about myself, I cannot talk about you. You know this as you listen to me, disappointment settling in your face.

MUSE

What I look at when I type is a poster: Edward Hopper's *Nighthawks*. It is there to keep me honest. I look at a couple having coffee in a diner late at night; their relationship is ambiguous; she looks fragile, vulnerable, no longer quite young; his forehead is shadowed by the wide brim of his hat. Their faces are bleached by the merciless light. The gaunt-faced waiter leans forward; he wants to tell them about himself. They are someone to talk to in this plate-glass house with the redundant salt and pepper shakers, the carefully spaced chrome napkin holders. The man apart, whose back is to me, is a mystery. Forty-five years ago, when Hopper painted these people, did he know they would endure? I see them downtown in the underground concourse below the glass hotel and the granite-and-marble bank, in that spooky region lined with overpriced shops selling cheap goods, and drab cafes tarted up with lights. There they are, no older, only he is hatless these days. The waiter-turned-waitress is still thin-faced and can't support her kids on what she makes. And the loner sits in the corner and faces me now, but his face might as well be a back.

SLIDES

My friend has no wish to travel. "I don't have to visit Las Vegas," he says. "I already know what it's like." Yes, and what the Sistine Chapel is like, and the Amazon jungles, the faces of Everest, and the Hall of Mirrors at Versailles, though he hasn't visited any of them. His head, like everyone else's, is a museum of places he has not been to, filled with color slides. He owns the Grand Canyon, the rock star's mansion, the treatment center where the First Lady was cured of alcoholism, the Great Wall of China. The only place he can't flatten into a two-dimensional image is the house that surrounds him: the gleaming bathtub that could turn treacherous, the kitchen filled to exploding with years of talk, the bed upstairs, at the moment pristine, tucked-in, that gives no hint of its intentions.

Brendel Playing Schubert

We bring our hands together
in applause, that absurd noise,
when we want to be silent. We might as well
be banging pots and pans,
it is that jarring, a violation
of the music we've listened to
without moving, almost holding our breath.
The pianist in his blindingly
white summer jacket bows
and disappears and returns
and bows again. We keep up
the clatter, so cacophonous
that it should signal revenge
instead of the gratitude we feel
for the two hours we've spent
out of our bodies and away
from our guardian selves
in the nowhere where the enchanted live.

ROMANTICS

Johannes Brahms and
Clara Schumann

The modern biographers worry
"how far it went," their tender friendship.
They wonder just what it means
when he writes he thinks of her constantly,
his guardian angel, beloved friend.
The modern biographers ask
the rude, irrelevant question
of our age, as if the event
of two bodies meshing together
establishes the degree of love,
forgetting how softly Eros walked
in the nineteenth century, how a hand
held overlong or a gaze anchored
in someone's eyes could unseat a heart,
and nuances of address not known
in our egalitarian language
could make the redolent air
tremble and shimmer with the heat
of possibility. Each time I hear
the Intermezzi, sad
and lavish in their tenderness,
I imagine the two of them
sitting in a garden
among late-blooming roses
and dark cascades of leaves,
letting the landscape speak for them,
leaving us nothing to overhear.

NOCTURNE

Sometimes, in the dead of night, I wake up in an immense hole of silence. Then I wait, with hope and dread, for the first sound to drop into it. Hope for something benign: the soothing background music of rain, or an owl's throaty signal. Dread of a wailing siren, or the telephone, which at this hour could bring me only a thick, demented voice, or the impersonal speech issuing from some desk of disaster. Last night, when it came, it was a sound of blessing, the rough-and-tumble bumping-together of freight cars in the switchyard down the road—that simple, artless coupling, and a long time later, the drawn-out, low-voiced hum of the train rolling down the single track. Sounds of work, of confidence in the night, in getting from here to there. Sounds of connection; sweet music. I lay there and listened to the moonless night fill up with sound until the darkness throbbed with a dream of arrival.

MY GRANDMOTHER'S GOLD PIN

"for the flowers I'd bring, if I could, to the grave on the
other side of a Wall which should be a metaphor or a bad dream/"

This poem was written two decades before the fall of Communism in Europe. The Cold War was on, and the Wall, which divided East Germany from West Germany, was a physical barrier confining the East Germans within their borders and making access by their families from the West difficult and often impossible.

BEGINNING WITH 1914

"we start in an obsolete country,
on no current map."

The assassination of Crown Prince Franz Ferdinand of Austria, the incident that led to World War I, occurred in 1914. He was killed in Sarajevo, the capital of Bosnia-Herzegovina, which was then a province of the Austro-Hungarian Empire. After the defeat of Austria, several provinces, including Bosnia-Herzegovina, were joined with Serbia to form the country of Yugoslavia. In the 1970s, when I wrote this poem, Yugoslavia was ruled by the Communist dictator Marshal Tito. In the service of a common Yugoslav nationality, ethnic differences were no longer recognized. As I write this note in 1995, three years into the war in Bosnia, it is hard to imagine that this region was ever erased, not only from maps but from historical consciousness.

THE TRIUMPH OF LIFE: MARY SHELLEY

"And in a few more decades,
when your test-tube babies sprout,"

Again, history has overtaken poems written during the early 1970s. At that time the first successful in vitro fertilization, though envisioned, was still presumed to be a long way off.